Dedication:

Nobody Said it was Easy...

Dr. J. D. Watson

BMH Books
P.O. Box 544
Winona Lake, Indiana 46590

This book about Dedication
is affectionately dedicated to:

My Saviour, whose love has redeemed *me;*
My wife, Debbie, whose help has reassured *me;*
And J. Sidlow Baxter, whose writings have refreshed *me.*

All Scripture quotations in this book, unless otherwise noted,
are from *The New Scofield Reference Bible*, copyright 1967
by Oxford University Press. Other quotations are from *The
American Standard Bible*, copyright 1960, 1962, 1963, 1968,
1971, 1972, 1973, 1975, 1977 by The Lockman Foundation.

COPYRIGHT 1987
BMH BOOKS
WINONA LAKE, INDIANA

Printed in U.S.A.

ISBN: 0-88469-181-0

Cover design by Hart and Hart

Table of Contents

Preface

It has been a pleasure to read through the chapters which comprise this book. The importance of its theme is beyond question. After our conversion to Christ the most far-reaching crisis is our utter self-yielding to Him. That is the crisis which opens the golden door to all those deeper, richer spiritual blessings which Christian hearts covet. That, also, is the center-point of this book, and it is dealt with in an earnest, able, challenging way by a gifted penman. True to the title of the book, the dedication here expounded is not presented as something easy or superficial, but as a deep-going act of mind and will, with transforming effects in Christian character. Every page is "right on the mark." Many a paragraph flashlights this or that or the other aspect. To the serious reader it can bring nothing but spiritual profit. May it have rich ministry.

— *Dr. J. Sidlow Baxter*

Introduction

WHY THIS BOOK WAS WRITTEN

Why write a book on dedication? Answer, because dedication is *everything*. Without an attitude of complete dedication to Christ, then our lives will be nothing at all for the glory of God. Without real dedication, all we shall do is live for ourselves and be controlled by this world.

The "Dedication Principle" is a *once-for-all dedication, or giving over, of our hearts and lives to the Lord Jesus Christ*. I have preached this truth in many churches and, as I state in Chapter 1, "This is a message I wish I could preach in every church in America." Well, obviously, I can't do that, so I felt burdened to write it down.

There are many Christians in our churches today who have never given themselves completely to the control of God. It is for this very reason that the attitudes of shallowness, complacency, indifference, immaturity, unfaithfulness, and worldliness permeate our churches and lives.

Like any book, the lay-out of this one is important. Part I lays the foundation by defining the "Dedication Principle" as it is presented in Romans 12:1 and 2, the two most foundational verses to living the Christian life.

Special care is taken to explain the three features of dedication in those two verses, *Presentation, Separation,* and *Transformation.* They show that every believer must give themselves totally to Christ in order to know real growth and victory. We'll then see how this principle is illustrated in the New Testament and that even the Old Testament teaches this principle of divine control.

Part II presents an indepth look at *Separation* from this world. It defines exactly what "this world" is from James 4 and 5 and shows what the Christian's relationship should be to it.

Part III is made up of additional chapters on *Transformation,* the deeper growth of the Christian. Important subjects such as the "Fruit of the Spirit," "Faithfulness," "Bible Study," "Prayer," and other encouragements are brought into focus.

All this is supplemented by two appendices. The first presents evidence for the believer's security in Christ, as this is only briefly discussed in Chapter 8. The second appendix is "The Christian's Library," a reprint of a tract containing recommended reading for *every* Christian.

I do suggest that this book not just be "read through." In other words, I don't think it should be read in a hurry. I suggest that no more than one chapter be read each day. There is a lot of material to think about and ponder, and quick reading will leave much behind.

In addition to this, a major attitude of the book is toward "self-examination." God tells us to "examine ourselves to see if we are in the faith and to prove ourselves" (1 Cor. 13:5). The reader is often encouraged, but also challenged and exhorted, to be exactly what God wants him (or her) to be.

As the book is read, I hope the "personal tone" is evident. It is meant to be. I constantly try by the Spirit's power to preach and teach the Word of God to God's people in a personal way, showing them (and myself) what God demands of us. In fact, the contents of this book are taken from my preaching ministry, for I strongly believe that there is no greater power than the expository preaching of God's Word. Therefore, except for minor changes for literary sake, what is here in print is what I have actually preached to many believers.

As I said, I often encourage, challenge, and exhort, and at times I make some strong statements. But I pray that none of this comes off as dogmatism or unkindness, for this would destroy the whole purpose of the book. At times some will disagree with something "controversial," but I ask that the reader always prayerfully ponder and see what God is saying to His people.

I do pray that the contents of this book will help Christians in their walk, for these same things have certainly helped me. May God bless you.

— *The Author*

PART I

THE DEDICATION PRINCIPLE

CHAPTER ONE

The Dedication
of the Believer

In Romans 12:1-2, we read:

I beseech you therefore, brethren, by the mercies of God, that
you present your bodies a living sacrifice, holy, acceptable unto
God, which is your reasonable service. And be not conformed to this
world, but be ye transformed by the renewing of your mind, that
you may prove what is that good, and acceptable, and perfect will of
God.

Now, the first thing that we see is that this text says "I beseech you *therefore.*" The word "therefore" links what has
already been said in Paul's letter with what is going to be said.
Let us briefly outline the Book of Romans.

The first section covers chapters 1-8 and is the "Doctrinal
Section" which shows how the Gospel saves the sinner. Chap-
ters 9-11 cover the "National Section" which shows how the
Gospel relates to Israel. Then in Chapters 12-16 we see the
"Practical Section" which shows how the Gospel relates to con-
duct.

That last section needs to be broken down a little further. In that section we see how the Gospel relates to conduct; first, in relation to ourselves (12:1-2); second, in relation to the church (12:3-8); third, in relation to society (12:9-12); fourth, in relation to government (13); and fifth, in relation to other believers (14:1−16:13).

That, "in a nutshell," is the Book of Romans. It is very important to have a basic grasp of Romans before we discuss Romans 12:1 and 2, for we cannot understand these two verses if we do not have this basic knowledge. The reason for this is that the thrust of these verses is what we would call "the total dedication of the believer to the will of God in his life." We see in these two verses Paul telling these people at Rome there is one thing that must come in their Christian lives before they can ever be victorious, before they can really be used of God, before they can ever see any real maturity, and that is, *a once-for-all dedication, or giving over of their hearts and lives to the Lord Jesus Christ.* This is what we call "The Dedication Principle."

This is a message which I wish I could preach in every church in America. The reason for this desire is because even though we often say that "eternal life" begins at salvation, the real "Christian life" does not begin until we are dedicated to Christ. I do not want to be misunderstood here for I am only being technical in my terms. At the moment we accept Christ into our lives we are born again, we have eternal life, and we are on our way to heaven. However, a real and vital "Christian life" has not begun until we say: "Lord, here is my whole life. You take it and use it for your glory and will." Everything hinges here. There must be in every believer's life a total once-for-all dedication of his life to Christ.

May we look at these two verses in a progressive manner. We will look first at the *reason* for our dedication (why we should be dedicated); second, at the *reality* of our dedication (how to go about being truly dedicated to Christ); and, third, at the *result* of our dedication (what comes out of this dedication).

I. THE REASON FOR OUR DEDICATION

In verse 1 we see the reason for our dedication and that this reason is twofold. However, we need to take note of that first phrase, "I beseech you." The word here from the Greek means "to entreat; implore"; and comes from the Greek word *parakaleo* which is the verb form of the noun *parakletos* (one who is called alongside to aid). This word is translated "comforter" in John 14:16, 26; 15:26; and 16:7, referring to the indwelling Holy Spirit; and "advocate" in 1 John 2:1, referring to the Lord Jesus Christ as our intercessor in heaven. Now the verb form tells us that Paul is "coming alongside of us" to implore us, to beseech us, to beg and to *plead* with us that we give our lives to Christ.

Beloved Christian, why is this so important? Why is Paul making a real effort to show how important this is? The *first* half of the reason is "because of the mercies of God," that is, because of all that God has done for us. As we look at what God has done for us, can we really comprehend what has been accomplished through the Lord Jesus Christ?

As we look at those first eleven chapters of Romans we see the justification we have in Christ. We have been "declared righteous" by the judicial act of God through the blood sacrifice of Christ. In Christ we have adoption, that is, we, who were once "children of darkness" and who were once, as the Pharisees, "of our father the devil" (John 8:44), we are now called "children of God" because of Christ (John 1:12). We have, through Christ, sanctification. We have been "set apart" *from sin* and *unto service*. We have in Christ that preservation and security knowing that nothing can separate us from the love of God.

Look at all we have in Christ! Paul says, in essence, "Based upon all this, I beseech you to present yourselves a living sacrifice." So, the first half of the reason is because of God's mercies.

The *second* half of the reason flows from the first. It is, therefore, our "reasonable service." The word "reasonable" comes from the Greek word *logikēn* where we get the word "logical" in English. As we look at the mercies of God, is it not indeed the logical thing to do to give the Lord Jesus Christ your life completely?

The reason for our dedication is very important and very plain. Paul said the reason you should give your life to Jesus is because He has given everything for you. Many believers these days say "but Preacher, it's my life to live. Yes, the Lord saved me, but I want control of my life now." The problem here is the fact that it is *not* our lives to live. Galatians 2:20 declares:

I have been crucified with Christ: nevertheless I live; yet not I but Christ liveth in me; and the life that I now live in the flesh [body] I live by the faith of the Son of God, who loved me and gave Himself for me.

Dear Christian, it's not your life to live. No matter what age you may be, it's not your life to live. Your life is in Christ and belongs to Him because He gave *His* life for *your* life.

Paul said, "I beseech you by the mercies of God," because it is the "reasonable response." Oh, may we give Him all of ourselves in one act of the will!

II. THE REALITY OF OUR DEDICATION

May we now look at the reality of our dedication. How can one have a truly dedicated Christian life? What is true dedication? Webster's Dictionary defines "dedicate" this way: "To set apart for some purpose, especially a religious one; devote." This is a good start, but God takes it far beyond this. We see in these two verses there are *three* features of true biblical dedication. We hear a lot of preaching on dedication, but do we hear it according to these two verses? We hear these verses quoted a lot, but are they being exposited according to the language and context? Notice these three features of true biblical dedication.

A. Presentation

Presentation is the first feature and it is found in that word "present." The Greek word *parastēsai* means "to place beside." To present something to someone is to literally pick it up and place it beside him. This is what Paul is pleading with the Christians in Rome to do. He is pleading with them to place themselves in the hands of the Lord Jesus Christ.

Now we come to the most important thought of this chapter, if not the whole book. Please set your mind on this one thought. The tense of this verb ("to present") is *not* a tense of present or continuous action as some are teaching today. Many dear brethren are teaching what is called "rededication," but there is no such scriptural teaching. There *is* a scriptural doctrine of *growth* which is what we shall examine in a few moments in the third feature of dedication, but "rededication" has no biblical foundation.

The verb here is in what is called the aorist tense, which in the Greek language is the simple past tense. If you do something in the aorist tense, you have done it one time and one time only. That action can *never* be repeated. No matter how long you live, there is only one point in time in the aorist tense. Therefore, Paul is saying, "I beseech you that in one irrevocable act of surrender, you present yourself once-for-all to Jesus Christ."

We need to fully understand what Paul means. Back in Romans 6:13 Paul uses the same word. He says "do not yield your members as instruments of unrighteousness to sin," and there he uses the present tense. Do not be "continually yielding" yourselves to sin, but "yield (aorist tense now) your members once-and-for-all as instruments of righteousness unto God."

There are many people today that are emphasizing the emotions and emphasizing "experience." However, Paul is emphasizing here, as he does throughout his epistles, the importance of the mind and the will in the believer. We'll come back to this truth in a moment, but Paul is emphasizing an irrevocable, irreversible act of the will.

Again, there are some dear brethren preaching "rededication." Some of them do it in innocence thinking that "presentation" is the same as "growth," but, as we have seen, it isn't. Still others teach rededication just to get people down the aisle of a local church so they can count it as "a decision." However, this is certainly not God's way. What we must see is that this *presentation* is the first feature of dedication which must be true in our lives.

I have come to call this one-time-act *the crisis point of dedication.* I did not say an "emotional point," an "emotional upheaval," an "emotional explosion," or an "experience on the mountaintop." I said a "crisis-point" in your life. This can be defined as *a definite point in time when you consciously and completely gave yourself over to divine control.*

Let us go through it again. A definite point in time (a distinct moment in your life that you remember) when you consciously (with your mind and will) and completely (totally and unconditionally) gave yourself over (surrender, yield, and submit) to divine control (the Holy Spirit's leading and God's will for your life apart from self-will).

That is a crisis point. It is nothing of which to be afraid. Everyone who is saved came to a crisis-point at salvation. Salvation is *not* just an emotional experience. The whole *personality,* which is made up of the intellect, the emotions, and the will, is involved in salvation. All three aspects of the personality are equally balanced. The intellect *knows* the truth of salvation, the emotions are *stirred* by the truth, and the will *acts* on the truth. It must also be this way in the life of the believer when it comes to this dedication of the life.

I would like to challenge you, the reader, to a decision right now. I dare say that many who read these pages can remember a moment in their lives when they said, "Lord, here is my life; you take my life and control it," in a once-for-all giving over to Christ. However, I would also dare say that many have never made that decision.

In many places that I have gone in recent years, I have seen people walking the aisles of local churches after a message on this principle has been preached. People who have been saved for twenty and thirty years, people who have been members of a Bible-preaching church for most of their Christian lives, have come to say, "Yes, Lord, here is my life." Why is this? Because there are many Christians today who have never been confronted with the exact meaning of real dedication.

Many say that dedication is reading the Bible, praying, and witnessing. True, all of these are *continuing factors* of maturity, but dedication *begins* with a once-for-all presentation and, Dear Christian, there are many who have *never* made that decision! The reason there is no consistency, no faithfulness, and no victory in many Christians' lives is because they have never said, "Lord, here is my life. You control it." They have the "reins of the horses" and are in control instead of allowing God to control.

In Chapter 3, we will look at a man named Saul, a man who not only had everything, but he also held (and would not let go of) the reins of his own life. His life ended in total defeat because of "self-will." The challenge is plain: Don't be like Saul, give your life totally to God's will and control. There *must* be that distinct time in your life.

Please note the rest of verse 1. It says present your *bodies* a living sacrifice. It does not say present your "soul" or your "spirit," because God already possesses these. But what He must have is your body, for that is what He is going to use, develop and mature. God also wants a *living* sacrifice. Many want to wait until they are old to serve the Lord, but God doesn't want a "dead sacrifice." He wants one with vitality, one He can use. God wants a sacrifice that is *holy,* a life that is manifesting holy living. And God wants a sacrifice that is *acceptable,* that is, one which is always pleasing Him. All of this is indeed "our reasonable service."

Beloved Christian, I preach this principle often and make the challenge then as I do now that you must *now* make the most important decision of your life as a believer. You will either say "yes" or "no" to total dedication. Has there been a distinct moment in your life when you said, "Lord, here is my life"? There are numerous illustrations in Scripture of this decision, many of which we will mention in the following chapters.

Have *you* made that decision?

B. Separation

The second feature of this dedication is *separation.* Verse 2 says, "Be not conformed to this world." The Greek word "conformed" literally means "to fashion in accordance with," that is, to fashion something to look like something else. In other words, the outward looks like the world, while the inward is converted.

Therefore, there is something hypocritical and two-faced. Paul uses the present tense here and the imperative mood (which shows a command) to literally say, "stop being continually conformed to this world." This is what he said in Chapter 6, verse 13.

God wants us to be "unfashionable" to this present world system. The word "world" refers to the system of this world, not the physical world. Therefore, God does not want us to have the attitudes, the actions, the motives, the desires, the values, the priorities, the inclinations, or the methods of this world system. We will look at this in more detail in Chapters 4 and 5, but what is meant by worldliness is an attitude of the mind and heart.

Paul is saying here, "stop being conformed to this present world system. Stop allowing the world to dictate. Stop being pressed into the mold of this world." Until we do this we are not living a dedicated Christian life. This is present tense, but until the once-for-all surrender (aorist tense) is true, then we'll never be able to be truly separate from the world.

These days many Christians try and try not to be "worldly." They do all the things their pastors say to do and they don't do anything the pastors say not to do. They, then, think that because of all that, they're going to be spiritual; but they still find they are not happy. Why? Because they aren't surrendered. They aren't consistent. They aren't faithful. Why? Because they have never said, "Lord, here is my life." Worldliness is *first* an attitude, then an action. If our attitude is in agreement with the world, we will then be worldly; but if we have given our lives totally to Christ, we will not have a worldly attitude. Again, we will come back to these thoughts in detail in later chapters.

C. Transformation

We come now to the last feature of true dedication, *transformation.* This also is a continuing work. "Do not be conformed to this world, but be transformed by the renewing of the mind." The word in the Greek for "transformed" is *metamorphoō* where we get the English word "metamorphosis." This word means "a change within, to change form." It speaks of something which is done on the inside, unlike "conformed" which speaks of something done on the outside.

A perfect example of a metamorphosis known to everyone is that of a butterfly. The little worm goes inside the cacoon and in a few weeks he comes out and is something completely different inside *and* out. Its nature is changed, its makeup is changed; everything about it has been transformed.

You see, what the world tries to do is to change the outside in order to change the inside. That's what *religion* tries to do, for religion is nothing more than what man tries to do in himself to get to God; while *Christianity* is what God has done for man. That's also what philosophy tries to do. However, the Word of God transforms the inside which *then* changes the outside. That is what God is continually doing in us.

This same idea is given in Matthew 17:2 "Christ was transfigured, and His face did shine as the sun." Have you ever noticed what happens to someone who gets saved? There is something that changes overnight. They're not fully mature (who is?), they're only newborn babes in Christ. However, *something* has changed. It's something that even shows on their face. The word used for "transfigured" is the same word used here for this "transformation." Do you see? God *will* do something in your life. When you present yourself to Christ once-for-all, remain separated from this world system, and have the desire to grow and mature in Christ, "your face will shine as the sun."

What a change it is that comes in the new Christian! However, so often it's the older Christians who sit back and ridicule the newer Christians who are excited with what God has done in their lives. Those old "prune-faced" Christians on the back rows of the church frown and cross their arms and say, "Oh, that excitement will wear off." Oh, may it never wear off! Never be a discouragement to those around you, for there *is* something that changes and if there is not something *continually* changing in you, you should realize there is something seriously wrong with your spiritual life. Read it again slowly: "His − face − did − shine − as − the − sun."

Note carefully the phrase "by the renewing of your mind," for it is here that we see *how* this transformation comes about. Paul again emphasizes the importance of the *mind.* There are so many today emphasizing the emotions and what God is going to do in our emotions and experience and that we've got to always be on the mountaintop or we're not spiritual. But in all of his epistles, Paul *never* emphasized the emotions as the thing which should control or the thing in which God is going to do His greatest work. He emphasized everywhere the importance of the believer's mind (Rom. 14:5; Phil. 1:27, 2:2, 4:7; 2 Tim. 1:7; etc.).

We have many "uneducated Christians" these days. They're not uneducated as far as the world is concerned, but they are as far as the Word of God is concerned. This "continual renewing of the mind" is what is going to aid us in being separate from the world. We are bombarded every moment of the day by the world—where we work, in our homes, by the newspapers, by magazines, and by television. What we *must* have is the continual renewing of the mind and it will only come by a deep involvement with the Word of God. This continuous transformation (growth) only comes through the Word.

This "transformation" is what many confuse with "rededication." Dedication is first of all a once-for-all decision of the mind. Once that presentation is made, the dedicated Christian life continues. We must understand that this "transforming" is the process of Christian growth. This subject will be often emphasized throughout this book. Christians *must* love the Word of God or they will not grow.

May we emphasize again, are you truly a dedicated believer? Has there been that moment that you gave your life to Christ? Are you now being unfashionable to this world system and being separate from it, not in *contact* but in *conformity* to its values, priorities, and philosophies? And are you continually being transformed by the renewing of your mind through God's Word?

Are *you* dedicated?

III. THE RESULT OF OUR DEDICATION

May we look now at the *result* of our dedication. What is going to happen when we have truly dedicated our lives to Jesus Christ? When we are presented once-for-all, when we are continually being unfashionable to this world system, and when we are continually growing and maturing in Christ through His Word, what is going to happen?

Verse 2 gives the answer, "that you may prove what is that good, and acceptable and perfect will of God." This is God's promise. However, many these days search for what to do in a particular situation without knowing there are prerequisites for finding the answer. We can't be led in the will of God if we aren't dedicated. It's *that* simple. If we are not presented, if we are not separated, and if we're not being transformed, we cannot be led in the will of God. It is an impossibility.

Many young people say they want to know the will of God, but they aren't dedicated. Many adults say they want to know the will of God but they aren't dedicated. They come to a difficulty and say, "Lord, what should I do?" They do not know because they aren't dedicated. It's not just the major decisions in life in which God will reveal His will, but it will be the "constant proving of His will" in *every* aspect of our lives (present tense).

It is easy to note how all of this ties together. A completely surrendered life which is continually deemphasizing the world and is constantly involved with the Word of God will be able to evaluate conduct, will be able to discern the Lord's leading in every situation, will be able to evaluate and discern the false doctrine that is prevalent today, and will manifest real wisdom and maturity. *This* is the result of real dedication.

Some may think, "Well, if I'm going to give my whole life to Christ, shouldn't God then in return give me something great like making me rich or famous? Shouldn't He give me something I can see?" Ponder this: *What could be greater or more valuable than knowing the will of God in every step you take?*

Note the adjectives that Paul uses. He says the "good" (or profitable) will of God. Many Christians are afraid of the will of God. They sit down and think of the most horrible thing and think that must be the will of God. God's will is always good and profitable. Akin to this is the next adjective "well-pleasing." When you are truly dedicated you will see what real joy is and what real peace is, because you'll be in the will of God. You *will* be pleased with God's will. God does not lead us into things that make us miserable. God's will is enjoyable. Then we see that Paul says God's will is "perfect." There are some today that are saying God doesn't have a specific will for the believer. However, according to the Scriptures, God's will is perfect, that is, as the Greek word *teleios* means, "mature, full-grown." God has something specific for *you.*

There are many young people who say, "Well, I know what I want to do in my life, where I want to go to school, and what I'm going to be." But, have they asked God? Many adults say, "Well, I'm in this vocation and I'm doing what I want to do." However, have they asked God if that is where He wants them? I have known many men of God who at one time were in a secular vocation as a Christian; but when they finally realized the meaning of real dedication, they quit that job and went to school, because God had called them to preach. It doesn't matter where we are now. What matters is where does God want us in the future?

We see in the Word of God that *salvation is free, but dedication costs everything.* It cost our Saviour everything. Even Jesus had to surrender His will. Yes, He was one hundred percent God, but He was also one hundred percent man and even He had to say "not my will, but Thine be done." The Saviour did not want to partake of "the cup" of separation from the Father, but the will of the Father was everything. If Jesus could say it, why can't we?

* * * * *

May we note that *everything* in these two verses is progressive (present tense), this separation, this transformation, this renewing of our minds, this proving of God's will are all progressive and continue. Everything is continuous *except one thing,* the once-for-all decision to present ourselves to Christ.

Dear Christian, it all begins right here. Have you given Christ the "reins of your life"? You can never know those things which are in the present tense until you settle what's in the aorist tense.

I read these words some years ago and have never forgotten them: "Lord Jesus, from now on my rule of life shall be—Thy will alone; nothing less, nothing more, at all costs" (J. Sidlow Baxter). Is this *your* prayer? Have you given Him everything?

CHAPTER TWO

The Dedication Principle in the New Testament

By now I hope it is clear to us what dedication really is and what we mean by "The Dedication Principle." It is a *once-for-all dedication, or giving over of our hearts and lives to Christ.* We have seen that this begins with a "crisis point" of *presentation* and continues in our *separation* from this world and our *trans formation* by the Word of God.

The purpose of this chapter (and the next) is to briefly study some additional illustrations from the Scriptures on this subject of total dedication. As we go through God's Word we cannot fail to be amazed at the frequency of this principle and see that God *never* used anyone who was not completely given over to divine control. God cannot use someone who is "partially dedicated." Though we cannot examine every illustration, let us look at a few New Testament examples of this most foundational truth.

I. THE LIFE OF CHRIST

The first illustration we *must* look at is that of our Saviour. He is the perfect example for our lives in *every* respect. There are many passages of Scripture which show His surrender of will, but perhaps the best is Chapter 2, verses 5-8 of Philippians:

> Let this mind be in you which was also in Christ Jesus. Who, being in the form of God, thought it not robbery to be equal with God. But made Himself of no reputation, and took upon Him the form of a servant, and was made in the likeness of men; and, being found in fashion as a man, He humbled Himself and became obedient unto death, even the death of the cross.

May we realize the surrender of Christ. He was *God* but came as a *man*. He was *King* but came as a *servant*. He was the *Creator* but came without *reputation*. He was eternally *alive* but came to *die*.

These verses shed great light on the scene in Matthew 26:39 where we find Christ agonizing in the Garden of Gethsemane. Christ knew that when He hung on the cross and took the sin of man upon Him, then the Father would have to turn His back and forsake Him. Jesus knew He would be saying those horrible words, "My God, My God, why hast Thou forsaken me?" (Matt. 27:46). So, as He prayed in the Garden, He asked, "O my Father, if it be possible, let this cup pass from me; nevertheless, not as I will, but as Thou wilt." The cup Jesus did not want to partake of was separation from God and He wished that the cup could pass from Him. However, He also knew salvation could only come if He "became sin for us" (2 Cor. 5:21), so He humbled Himself to the most hideous and degrading death known to man—crucifixion.

We see then that even Christ had to surrender His will. But why? He was God. Yes, but not only was He one hundred percent God, but He was also one hundred percent man and *every man* must surrender his will. Jesus did, and so must we.

II. THE LIFE OF PAUL

When we first see Paul, his name is Saul, and he is one of the main persecutors of the early believers in the Book of Acts. However, when Saul came to Christ he totally gave his life to the will of God. We see the first reference to his dedication in Acts 9:20 as he "immediately preached Christ in the synagogues."

However, to really find Paul's dedication we must go to his epistles. First, we note Philippians 3:7-10:

> But what things were gain to me, those I counted loss for Christ. Yea doubtless, and I count all things but loss for the excellency of the knowledge of Christ Jesus, my Lord; for whom I have suffered the loss of all things, and do count them but refuse, that I may win Christ. And be found in Him, not having mine own righteousness, which is of the law, but that which is through the faith of Christ, the righteousness which is of God by faith. That I may know Him and the power of His resurrection, and the fellowship of His sufferings . . . .

This is one of my favorite passages to ponder and preach and I wish we could delve deeply into it, but we can only look at it briefly now and once again in Chapter 6. However, we see here Paul's dedication to Christ. The whole attitude of the passage shows Paul's *presentation* of life, that nothing mattered to him except Christ. We then also can see his *separation* from the world as he counted the worldly goods and possessions as "refuse." We also see his *transformation,* that continuing growth in Christ, in his constant desire to know more and more of Christ through His Word.

We then go to 2 Timothy 1:12:

> For which cause I also suffer these things; nevertheless, I am not ashamed; for I know whom I have believed and am persuaded that He is able to keep that which I have committed unto Him against that day.

The word translated "committed" is a Greek word which is similar to the word used for "present" in Romans 12:1. However, the fascinating thing about the word here is that it is not a verb as the King James translation implies. It is actually a *noun* and its literal translation would be, "He is able to guard my deposit." Paul knew that he had "deposited" his life in God's hands and was allowing God to control.

Then in 2 Timothy 2:4, we read:

> No man that warreth entangleth himself with the affairs of this life, that he may please him who hath chosen him to be a solider.

The word "chosen" comes from a Greek word which literally

means "to enlist troops." The enlisted soldier no longer lives according to his own will. He surrenders his will to the commander's will. Neither does the soldier entangle himself in other things, but separates himself from anything which would effect his service for the commander.

As we continue in 2 Timothy, we find a well-known verse:

> Study to show thyself approved unto God, a workman that needeth not to be ashamed, rightly dividing the Word of Truth (2:15).

The word "study" comes from a word that actually means "eager," and the words "to show" come from the same Greek word used in Romans 12:1 for "present." Paul is here encouraging Timothy, and us, to "be eager to present ourselves unto God's *will* and God's *Word.*

Paul then adds in 2 Timothy 3:10 that "thou hast fully known . . . my purpose." The word used for "purpose" is yet another word which means "setting before," but is here used as a noun, therefore, picturing an *object* which has been set before something or someone else. Paul is telling us that his life is the object which has been set before God so that He can control it.

Elsewhere in Paul's writings we find one of the most important Scriptures in all of the Word of God concerning the Holy Spirit. This Scripture is 1 Thessalonians 5:19:

> Quench not the Spirit.

Some do not understand the difference between "quenching" the Holy Spirit and "grieving" the Holy Spirit. Ephesians 4:30 tells us not to grieve the Holy Spirit, and by the context (vv. 25-32) we see that we grieve Him by allowing sin into our lives. When we sin, we grieve (that is, sadden or bring pain) the Holy Spirit. However, to quench the Holy Spirit means, "to extinguished, dampen, or hinder the Holy Spirit." There is only one way man can extinguish or dampen the Spirit's work and that is to say, "No." Unyieldedness to the Holy Spirit and an unsurrendered life quenches His working in us.

III. THE LIVES OF THE DISCIPLES

Next, let us look at the twelve disciples and notice the dedication in their lives. We can see four of them in the passage in Matthew 4:18-22. The Lord Jesus calls Peter and Andrew with the words "Follow me" which come from a word which speaks of a command "to come." He then came to James and John and "called them." We don't know the words He used to call them, but we do discover by examining the word "called" that it is in the aorist tense. Jesus is, therefore, making a once-for-all call and wants a once-for-all decision to follow. We are then told that all four men *left* their nets and ships and *followed* Jesus. Both words are in the aorist tense showing a complete, once-for-all break with the past life and a giving over of their lives to Christ.

When Matthew was called to follow, his decision was the same as the previous four disciples. When Jesus called him to follow, "he arose, and followed Him" (Matt. 9:9) in a once-for-all decision.

We then see Philip being called with the same words in John 1:43, and, though his answer is not recorded, his life still shows us that he was indeed a surrendered man. As for Bartholomew, Thomas, James the Less, Thaddaeus, Simon, and Judas Iscariot, there is no direct mention of their calling other than being listed as "one of the twelve." However, except for Judas, each one was used of the Lord, possibly in a lesser degree than some of the other disciples, but still used. This indicates they were totally dedicated, for God does not use those who are not totally dedicated.

IV. THE LIFE OF PETER

Special mention needs to be made of Peter. The reason for this is that in John 21 we see Peter back in his old vocation after leaving it behind "once-for-all" in Matthew 4:20. This may cause some to wonder, but I think this is easily answered. We do see that Peter was totally surrendered to Christ at his call to service in Matthew, but we must also remember that Peter denied the Lord Jesus three times, so in John 21 we see Peter so full of guilt and grief, because of what he had done, that at this time he truly felt he had disqualified himself for service to Christ. Though he knew he had dedicated himself to Christ, he never thought Jesus would now want him as a disciple.

This fits the context for two reasons. First, when Jesus asked Peter, "Peter, do you love me?" He used the Greek word *agapaō* which speaks of a divine, selfless, all-giving love. However, in Peter's guilt he couldn't bring himself to use this word, so, when he answered, "Yes, Lord, Thou knowest that I love you," he used the Greek word *phileō* which speaks of a tender affection. The second reason is that we see Jesus "recommission" Peter three times in verses 15-17. He says, literally, "Feed my lambs," "Tend my sheep," and "Feed my sheep," each of which emphasizes a different responsibility. In doing this Jesus assures Peter that he *is* qualified to serve and should be doing so instead of fishing. Peter had surrendered his life to Christ, but (just like us) the Lord still needed to work in his life to constantly develop and transform him.

V. THE LIFE OF MARY OF BETHANY

I do wish we had ample space to examine the dedication to Christ shown to us by Mary of Bethany in Mark 14:3-9. However, not to mention her would be a great mistake. Mary came to anoint the Lord Jesus for burial, for she understood who He was and why He came, and her act was one of the most beautiful in all the Scriptures. There is much we could look at, but we'll just meditate upon the four characteristics of her act which illustrate her real dedication.

First, Mary knew it was not enough to just *desire* something *from* Christ, but that she must also *dedicate* something *to* Christ. In like manner, we have many today who talk about "all we have in Christ" and many say how much they love God. However, while we have much service of *lip* we have little dedication of *life*. Very few Christians today have actually fully given themselves to Christ. Oh, they talk about it, but they never do it.

Second, Mary realized "the cheap" was not enough, she had to dedicate the *most costly*. The ointment that Mary used was spikenard which came from an herb in the Indies. It was rare, difficult to obtain, and, obviously, very expensive. It was used to perfume the body, and, like all women, Mary wanted to be perfumed. However, Mary wanted to show her love for Jesus and, therefore, gave the most precious thing she owned. What an illustration of the *living sacrifice* that God wants us to be!

Third, Mary understood that a portion was not enough, she

had to dedicate it *all*. She didn't keep part of it for herself, she gave it all to Jesus. Likewise, Christ doesn't want part of us. Neither does He want the *left-overs*. He must have all of us or He cannot use us. When Romans 12:1 says, "present your bodies," it means the whole body.

Fourth, Mary saw that "the unbroken" was not enough, she had to dedicate *once-for-all*. Perhaps the most fascinating thing in this incident was that Mary had to break the vial to get to the ointment. The vial was made of alabaster which is a species of marble, and was used for preserving precious ointments. Its beautiful white color rendered it translucent, and, like the oil inside, it was expensive. However, all this didn't matter to Mary, for she was giving it all to Jesus. When Mary *broke* that vial she showed this to be a once-for-all gift to Jesus, never to be given again. It didn't matter who murmured against her (v. 5), for she was giving the most precious thing she owned to the most precious One who has ever lived—Jesus.

VI. THE LIFE OF A LITTLE BOY

Another incident which never ceases to bless my heart each time I read it or preach it is when a little lad gave his little lunch to the Living Lord who then used it to feed five thousand people. That little boy had no idea what Jesus was going to do with his lunch. All he knew was that Jesus must be hungry after teaching most of the day, so, he wanted Jesus to eat, even if he did not.

How instructive this is for Christian parents today! Many parents want their children and young people to be educated and want them to learn how to make a living, but they are unconcerned about whether or not their offspring know what it means to give their lives to Christ. Many parents are thrilled when their son (or daughter) is an athlete, but they don't care whether or not that son (or daughter) has dedicated his life to the will of God. Undoubtedly, the reason for this is that these parents are themselves undedicated Christians. Oh, may we teach our young people that there is nothing more important than a life surrendered to Christ.

In Mark's account of this incident, we are told that Jesus did four things with that little lad's lunch. Note Mark 6:41:

And when he had taken the five loaves and the two fishes, he looked up to heaven, and blessed and broke the loaves, and gave them to his disciples to set before them; and the two fishes he divided among them all.

First, we see that Jesus *took* it. What a blessing to know that whatever we offer, He takes. Our Lord is ready and willing to accept our lives as we offer them, but the question remains—"Are we willing to give?" Second, Jesus then *blessed* it. God will only bless those who have given themselves to His will. Third, Jesus *broke* it. Jesus must increase and we must decrease. Our will and our desire must be humbled, and there will be times when He will truly have to break us down in order to build us up the way He wants us. Fourth, Jesus then *used* it. That lunch could not be used the way it was: neither can we be used the way we are. God can only *use* us when He *has* us.

CHAPTER THREE

The Dedication Principle in the Old Testament

Let us now look at the "Dedication Principle" as it is illustrated in the Old Testament. While our Old Testament illustrations are, of course, not based upon an application of that New Testament text in Romans 12:1 and 2, we still see that true dedication is the giving over of the whole person to divine control. There is no "Testament barrier," nor "dispensational barrier," nor any other barrier to this basic and universal principle of total dedication to the will of God. Again, we will not be able to look at every illustration, but we can look at a number of "high-points."

I. THE LIFE OF SAUL

Up to now we have looked mainly at "positive" illustrations, that is, those who *did* give their lives over to divine control. However, our first Old Testament illustration shows us the tragedy which comes when we *don't* surrender our lives to divine control.

King Saul was a remarkable man, but when we look at his life as a whole we see one of the most tragic pictures in all of God's Word. We note first his *Rise* in 1 Samuel 9-12. Never did a man have more going for him than did Saul. He had a striking physique as well as a commendable disposition. Saul was a man who possessed great natural abilities, good character, and godly influence from men with whom he associated. We see him rise to be the first king of Israel.

However, something went wrong, for in 1 Samuel 12-15 we see Saul's *Rebellion*. We can easily see the outward manifestations of rebellion in three ways: he was *impatient* (12:8-13) as he did not wait for Samuel as God had told him to do; he was *impetuous* (14) as he without humility or godly motive imposed a "false fast" upon the people; and he was *insolent* (15) as he willfully disobeyed God and then lied in order to cover his sin.

However, there was an *inward* problem which caused these *outward* manifestations. Saul's inward problem is shown in many places, but note 1 Samuel 15:17:

> And Samuel said, when thou wast little in thine own sight, wast thou not made the head of the tribes of Israel, and the Lord anointed thee king over Israel?

Saul's problem was that he was no longer "little in his own sight." His problem was *self-will.* He put his will above God's will.

We often hear it said that we must "die to self," but, if I may get a little technical in terminology, it is not "self" to which we must die but to *self-ism.* Self is what we are, our personality, which is made up of intellect, emotion, and will. What we must "die to," or get rid of, is selfism, which is putting our will before God's will. This was Saul's problem—selfism. This selfism is the exact opposite of total dedication and it is that unyielding "no" we say to God.

Let us look briefly at the four steps of selfism. This attitude of putting our will above God's always takes these four steps:

First, there is "self-sensitiveness." This is the attitude of always being *aware* of our own needs, feelings, and desires. Many people are always aware of how they feel and what they want, but they never think about what God wants or never think about the needs of other people around them.

Second, there comes "self-assertiveness." This is the attitude of always *expressing* our needs, feelings, and desires. This is one of the most prevalent philosophies today. Many books teach us how to be self-assertive and many of the books and authors claim to be "Christian." We have prevalent today "success motivation" books and seminars which also are often promoted by Christian leaders. However, nowhere does God's Word instruct us to be self-assertive, but rather to be Christ-assertive.

Third, there follows "self-centeredness" which is the attitude of always *fulfilling* our needs, feelings, and desires. This follows logically, for when we are constantly aware of ourselves and constantly expressing ourselves, then we will constantly be fulfilling what we want. Someone who is self-centered didn't start out that way. The other two steps came first.

The fourth step of selfism is one which never enters our minds. It is "self-destructiveness." This is the result of *paying* for our needs, feelings, and desires. "Be sure your sin will find you out" (Num. 32:23). The result which comes from selfism is our own defeat, despair, and destruction.

This leads us to the last stage in Saul's life, his *Ruin* in 1 Samuel 27-31. The ruin in Saul's life is incredibly tragic. He stoops so low that he goes to a medium (fortune-teller) which was strictly forbidden. He continued in his self-will and ended up taking his own life in total disgrace.

The lesson we learn from Saul is plain: *Success, victory, and blessing come only through the complete surrender and obedience to the will and Word of God.* Saul had everything going for him: looks, talent, money, fame, position, strength. However, what killed him and disgraced him was *self-will.* He never surrendered his will.

Perhaps the greatest tragedy of Saul is found in 1 Samuel 26:21:

> Then said Saul, I have sinned . . . behold, I have played the fool, and have erred exceedingly.

Saul admitted his foolishness, but he did nothing about it. He stayed on that road to self-destructiveness.

Likewise, there are Christians today who are "playing the fool," because they are self-willed, undedicated, and disobedient. Oh, let us not play the fool.

This subject of self-will will be examined again in detail in Chapter 5.

II. THE LIFE OF GIDEON

When we think of Gideon we usually think of one of the great champions of the faith, but Gideon did not start out as a hero. When we first see him, he is *carnal* and unbelieving (Judges 6:11-17). He thought the Lord had forsaken His people and doubted God's power in delivering them. We can see in Gideon that the reason for carnality, that is, that which pertains to self apart from Spirit-control, is simple, basic unbelief. We are *carnal* when we do not take God at His Word.

Nevertheless, if we take this one more step, we can also see the cause of unbelief. The attitude which produces unbelief is looking at circumstances instead of looking to God. Peter looked at circumstances when he was walking on the water. The ten spies looked at circumstances. Therefore, the whole principle is this: "carnality is caused by unbelief which in turn is caused by taking our eyes off God and looking at this world."

We then see Gideon *consecrated* (Judges 6:18-27). God convinces Gideon and Gideon follows. He made a total break with the past and built an altar which was the "outward symbol" of an "inward transaction." He named that altar Jehovah-Shalom, Jehovah is my peace. How significant this is, for peace is what we have when we surrender ourselves to divine control. He proved he was surrendered by tearing down the idols of Baal, even though it could have cost him his life. Yes, Gideon was now totally dedicated, and because of that *act* of surrender God used him and three hundred well-chosen men to free the Israelites from Midian.

How many believers today have never built that spiritual altar of peace?

III. THE LIFE OF DAVID

David is truly a remarkable biblical character. We know him

as a shepherd, a warrior, and a king. There is much we could say about him, but may we just point out that David was without doubt a totally dedicated servant of God.

For example, note Psalm 37:3-5, 7:

> Trust in the Lord, and do good . . . .
> Delight thyself also in the Lord . . . .
> Commit thy way unto the Lord . . . .
> Rest in the Lord and wait patiently for Him . . . .

David here gives us "the four greatest attitudes." The one we immediately notice is "commit thy way unto the Lord." The Hebrew word used here for commit literally means, "roll thy way upon the Lord." This is what real commitment is—laying ourselves and our will upon the Lord and giving Him everything that He may have full control. David's emphasis here is *presentation.*

We then note, "rest in the Lord." The meaning here is, "to be refreshed; not the rest of inactivity, but the harmonious working of all the faculties and affections." The remainder of verse 7 reads:

> . . . fret not thyself because of him who prospereth in his way, because of the man who bringeth wicked devices to pass.

Is this not an encouragement to *separation?* God does not want us to be concerned with this world and the people in it. He wants us to rest in Him. He wants our "affection" to be in "the things of heaven, not on the things of the earth" (Col. 3:2).

We also notice the words "delight thyself in the Lord." The meaning of this is "to rejoice or be happy in something with others." Is David not now speaking of *transformation?* Do we really delight in God's Word, God's will, and God's work? Are we growing in Christ and being transformed by a constant involvement with Him?

We find these same thoughts in Psalm 119:112, which, even though it is not a psalm of David, still it instructs us to dedication:

> I have inclined mine heart to perform thy statutes always, even unto the end.

Here again is real once-for-all surrender and *presentation* of life. The Hebrew word used here for "incline" is most challenging. Its basic meaning is "to stretch or spread out; to bend away." It is applied to many things, one of which is "to cause to yield." The challenge to us is to *cause* our hearts to yield to God's will. It does not come easy, for it violates our own desire and fleshly will, but this is what God demands. Moreover, it is a once-for-all decision in that we cause our hearts to yield to Him "always."

Separation is then in view in verse 115:

> Depart from me, ye evildoers; for I will keep the commandments of my God.

And then in verses 113-117 we see that marvelous *transformation* through God's Word:

> ... Thy law do I love.
> ... I hope in Thy Word.
> ... I will keep the commandments of my God.
> Uphold me according unto Thy Word, that I may live ....
> Hold Thou me up, and I shall be safe; and I will have respect unto Thy statutes continually.

No discussion of David would be complete without mention of Psalm 51, that classic psalm of penitence for sin and restoration to fellowship. The psalm has three applications: *Personal,* for it is David's path to restored fellowship; *prophetic,* for it will be the pathway which Israel will take to be restored to fellowship with Jehovah as spoken of in Deuteronomy 10:1-10 which gives the conditions Israel must meet to enter the Promised Land under the Palestinian Covenant; and *practical,* for it shows the steps every believer must take to come back into full communion with God when sin enters his life.

At present, we can only touch briefly on these steps to restored fellowship. Note David's *self-examination* (v. 3) as he "acknowledges his transgression" and admits his sin. Note then his *shedding of sin* (vv. 1-5, 13) as his whole attitude is to renounce sin and be purged of it. Look then at his *sincere worship* (vv. 14-15) as he realizes that it is God who he has sinned against and it is God who must be worshiped and not offended. Notice his *submission* (vv. 16-17) for his heart is broken before God. Note the *Spirit-control* (vv. 11-12), for David never wanted to be without God's power in his life. Note also David's *service* (v. 13) as he greatly desired to "convert" and "teach" others concerning Jehovah.

However, for our purposes we will look closely at verses 16-17:

> For Thou desirest not sacrifice; else would I give it: Thou desirest not in burnt-offering. The sacrifices of God are a broken spirit: a broken and contrite heart, O God, Thou will not despise.

We see something here which is most fascinating. Verse 16 speaks of *outward observance*; while verse 17 speaks of *inward obedience*. Verse 16 shows an *outward action;* while verse 17 shows an *inward attitude.* Verse 16 pictures an *outward display;* while verse 17 pictures an *inward dedication.* We see this because the Hebrew word used here for "broken" is a word which means "to break, fracture, or shatter into pieces."

As we saw in the last chapter in the illustration of the feeding of the multitude, God never uses anything until He breaks it. David was truly broken for what he had done and is here coming back into submission. As we compare this with what we have already seen in Psalm 37, may we submit that in Psalm 37 we truly see a complete once-for-all presentation to God and that here in Psalm 51 we do not see a "rededication," but rather a *remembering* of what has already transpired in David's life.

The capstone to all this is found in another of David's psalms:

> Teach me to do Thy will . . . ; for Thou art my God (Ps. 143:10).

God is trying to teach us to do His will. The question is, "Are we willing to learn?"

Teach me, O Lord, to do Thy will;
Teach me to remember Golgatha Hill.
Teach me, O Lord, Thy ways to yearn;
Teach me, O Lord, to be willing to learn.

IV. THE LIFE OF MEPHIBOSHETH

One of the most beautiful stories in all of God's Word is found in the ninth chapter of 2 Samuel. It is the story of how King David, because of his love for Jonathan, wanted to show kindness to someone in King Saul's lineage. The person he found was Mephibosheth, Jonathan's crippled son. The parallels that we see in this chapter are amazing. Mephibosheth illustrates man and how he is graciously dealt with by God who is illustrated by King David.

Space does not allow a thorough examination of the chapter, but it is necessary to see these parallels in order to see how Mephibosheth was dedicated. The reader is urged to read the entire chapter of 2 Samuel 9 before he continues with the reading of this book.

We first see that Mephibosheth was crippled by a fall (1 Samuel 4:4); just as all of us were crippled by Adam's fall and are lost, lame, and lifeless. We then see it was King David's desire to show kindness (1 Samuel 9:1). What an example of God's grace, that unmerited favor to those who are lost! This kindness was for "Jonathan's sake"; just as God's grace to us is for the sake of Jesus, His Son. This kindness was not earned by Mephibosheth; just as we cannot earn salvation. Mephibosheth was sought for by the King (vv. 1, 5); just as God *always* seeks men and not the other way around. King David then sent others to fetch Mephibosheth (v. 5), and in so doing gave us a marvelous picture of evangelism. When Mephibosheth was brought before the King, he reverenced him (v. 6); unlike many today who have no reverence nor respect for God, God's house, God's Word, nor God's men. Mephibosheth then offered himself to be a servant of the King, as we are also to surrender ourselves to God. Mephibosheth then received riches (v. 7); just as we have received and will receive the inheritance which is in Christ. He was also given security, for he ate at the King's table "continually"; and likewise the same grace that *saved* us is the same grace that *keeps* us. Mephibosheth was also made a son of David (v. 11); just as we are made adopted sons because of Christ, the only begotten Son of God.

With this scene in mind, note again verse 6:

> Now when Mephibosheth, son of Jonathan, the son of Saul, was come unto David, he fell on his face and did reverence. And David said, Mephibosheth. And he answered, behold, thy servant.

Here is a perfect example of real surrender. The amazing thing to see is that Mephibosheth knew he was worthless and helpless. He refers to himself in verse 8 as a "dead dog," something which was truly abhorrent to a Jew. However, still he says "Behold thy servant." Quite often it's those who are the least talented that serve God the most, for they already know their unworthiness, while the talented ones often think they have a lot to offer to God. However, on the contrary, we are worthless in ourselves and it is only because "He has made us able ministers" (2 Cor. 3:6) that we are worthy to serve God.

There are many Christians today who have never said, "Behold thy servant." Until they do, they will never really grow in the Lord as He would desire.

V. WHAT BRINGS REVIVAL?

To close the first part of our study on the "Dedication Principle" may we look at the fact that *real* revival will never come in our churches unless believers are completely dedicated to Christ in the ways we have seen described. We sometimes hear these days talk about revival, although not nearly enough. From time to time we hear a sermon about it, but, for the most part revival is not *really* preached these days because of what it demands. Let's look at a few instances from God's Word which show us that total dedication is absolutely essential for revival to happen.

A. The Words of Isaiah

The prophet Isaiah defines revival for us in Isaiah 44:21-22:

Remember these, O Jacob and Israel; for thou art my servant ... thou shalt not be forgotten by me. I have blotted out, like a thick cloud, thy transgressions ... return unto me; for I have redeemed thee.

This shows us that, simply stated, revival is "a remembrance and returning to a former state," or we may put it another way, "a renewing of the mind and heart in such a way that we return to those things which God desires."

It is very distressing that many churches these days hold so-called "revival meetings" which in reality are nothing but evangelistic crusades in which they try to draw the unsaved to hear the Gospel. While there are times when the unsaved will come to church, and at that time should hear the Gospel, we must still realize that the church is for Christians and is the place they should be fed. Likewise, revival is first and foremost a "remembrance and returning" of Christians to the state in which they should be found.

Isaiah also tells us that real revival involves three things:

Cry aloud, spare not, lift up thy voice like a trumpet, and show my people their transgression, and the house of Israel their sins. Yet they seek me daily, and delight to know my ways, as a nation that did righteousness, and forsook not the ordinances of justice; they take delight in approaching God (Isa. 58:1-2).

Revival first involves a *conviction of sin* (v. 1). The word "show" means to put before or to expose. Sin must be exposed and put before our eyes that we may see that the problem is with us. In the words of Peter, "the time has come that judgment must begin in the house of God" (1 Peter 4:17).

Revival also involves a *consciousness of obedience to God* (v. 20). It is here we really see the returning to what we are supposed to be and do. Real revival is going to involve the desire to obey God and His Word.

Lastly, revival involves a *commitment to God's will* (v. 2b). To truly "delight in approaching God" one must be totally dedicated to God. It is very important to see that Isaiah is in these two verses, and the five verses which follow, exposing Israel's hypocrisy. They have only a form of godliness and are only going through the "religious motions." Likewise, there are many Christians who are only going through the motions and have never really surrendered themselves to God in order to live a dedicated life.

B. The Revival under Ezra and Nehemiah

We all remember the story of Nehemiah and how he led the people of Israel to rebuild the walls of Jerusalem which were still in ruins after the seventy-year Babylonian captivity. We all have read that marvelous verse in Nehemiah 4:6:

So built we the wall, and all the wall was joined together to half its height; for the people had a mind to work.

However, do we realize what this spirit of dedication really brought about? Yes, we know that an estimated two and one half miles of wall were built in fifty-two days (Neh. 6:15), but do we know what even greater work was done through this dedication?

I ask this because we see recorded in Nehemiah 8:1 to 10:39 one of the greatest revivals in all the Word of God. Again, space does not allow a full treatment of this passage, but we see there were four things which brought about that great revival under

Ezra. They were the preaching of the Word of God (chap. 8), prayer and fasting (9:1), confession of sin (9:2), and worship (9:3). The clear implication to all this is the fact that the people were surrendered to God both for physical labor on the walls and spiritual awakening in their hearts.

C. "That Great Revival Text"

Most Christians are familiar with that often quoted revival text in 2 Chronicles 7:14:

> If my people, who are called by my name, shall humble themselves and pray, and seek my face, and turn from their wicked ways, then will I hear from heaven, and will forgive their sin and heal their land.

When we examine this verse we find there are seven principles in it concerning revival. As we know the number seven is used in God's Word as a symbol of *perfection* and we see that this verse truly shows us how we can have a "perfect revival." Breaking it down even further, we see that when man does four things (as four is the number of the world and weakness), then God will do three things in return (for three is the number of God).

The main point to be considered is that the first thing man must do is *humble himself.* The Hebrew word used here means "to depress pride" and, therefore, pictures the meaning of real submission and surrender. It is the emptying ourselves of ourselves and giving that empty vessel to God so He may fill it and use it as He wills.

* * * * *

In this first part of our study I have tried to define and illustrate "The Dedication Principle" as God's Word presents it. Much more could have been said, but this should be enough for us to realize that "though eternal life begins at salvation, the real Christian life begins when we are dedicated."

PART II

MORE
ABOUT
SEPARATION

CHAPTER FOUR

What Is Worldliness?

In James 4:4, we read:

> Ye adulterers and adulteresses, know ye not that the friendship with the world is enmity with God? Whosoever, therefore, will be a friend of the world is the enemy of God.

We have from time to time in our study looked at separation and what it means. However, at this point it is essential that we understand exactly what worldliness is so that we may indeed know from what we are to be separated. There is no better place to be found to examine this subject than in James, Chapters 4 and 5.

Chapter 4 will lay a solid foundation of what God's Word means when it speaks of "this world." The next chapter will then build upon that foundation as it will show how we can be cured of worldliness.

The main thing we want to look at from God's Word is *attitude.* We need to look at the "attitude of worldliness" which produces the "actions of worldliness." Quite often people are concerned only with outward actions. However, what we need to examine are the attitudes we have which produce the acts we do. And, as we'll examine in a few moments, these attitudes involve our real values, desires, and priorities.

I do want it to be understood that this section of our study will not be a list of "do's and don'ts." We have too much of that already in many churches. What I want us to be concerned with is what our text says about our "friendship." The word used here is the word *philos* which means "a tender affection." God does not want our affections and desires turned toward this world; for when they are, we have, therefore, turned away from loving Him.

I would like to break this chapter down into two basic thoughts. First, we need to see what the "world" is and see how this relates to Christians. Second, I would like to present a very special illustration of worldliness called "Humanism" and show its prevalence in not only American society, as many Christian leaders are proclaiming, but also in the lives of Christians as well.

I. WHAT WORLDLINESS IS

What do we mean when we speak of the world, or worldliness? First of all, may we clearly see what it is *not*. There is that old saying which is, "I am not worldly and am, therefore, spiritual since I don't smoke, I don't drink, and I don't chew; and I don't run around with people that do." However, this is not what God's Word teaches; for, again, this shows only action—outward *display*, but no inward *delight*.

Worldliness has nothing to do with either what we do or do not do. The same is true of spirituality. Nothing we do makes us spiritual. We must first be spiritual before we can manifest spirituality. We must not "get the cart before the horse." When we are truly spiritual, there will be things that we will do and things we won't do, but none of those things *makes* us spiritual.

So, then, what is worldliness? In our text is the word "world." This word comes from the Greek *kosmos* which carries the basic meaning of "an order or system." It has a number of meanings in the New Testament depending on the context in which it is used. It can mean mankind, earthly possessions, that which is at enmity with God; or even a metaphor for sin as it appears in James 3:6, "world [or system] of iniquity."

However, in most instances the word *kosmos* carries the idea of the "world system" or "world order." And it is in this usage that we find the real definition of the world and worldliness. In examining a number of old Greek authorities, we find a most fascinating definition. Later in the chapter we will see why this definition is so amazing, but, for now, let us concentrate on the meaning of this "world system"; *"That order of things which is alienated from God and in which man is the center as he opposes God and His revelation."*

This order is one which opposes God and everything God stands for and propagates its own order. Furthermore, we see that this system which fights God is *the system of the devil.* He is "the Prince of the Power of the Air" (Eph. 2:2). This world became his domain when he was cast from heaven (Isa. 14:12-17). Man is the *center* of this world system, but Satan is the *head* of the system. Man is the one who is emphasized as supreme, but Satan is the one in control.

What we need to realize is that this world system in which we live has been designed by and is controlled by Satan. At the heart of the system is *Satan's attitudes, motives, desires, priorities, values, methods, and inclinations.* In other words, that which is the opposite of God's attitudes, motives, desires, priorities, values, methods, and inclinations is worldly and is of Satan's system.

Dear Christian, *this* is the order of Satan. He is trying to weave this system into our lives as believers and in many cases he is doing a good job of it. This system is diametrically opposed to God, it is the exact opposite. And it is with this in mind that James says, "whoever is a friend of the world is the enemy of God." Those who have a tender affection for the world, those who are in love with the world, those who are compatible with the world, those who "fit-in" with the world are the enemies of God!

At this point I want to take those attitudes of this world system which we mentioned earlier (the motives, desires, values, and so forth) and state them in a little different fashion which should be somewhat easier to remember. We should have no friendship with this world system in *six* particular areas.

A. The <u>Philosophy</u> of This World System

This first area really encompasses all the others. Everyone lives according to a particular philosophy, a standard or guideline which rules the life. Put simply, the philosophy of this world is that man is *first, foremost, and final.* The philosophy Satan wants to spread is that man is "it," man is everything, man doesn't need God, man can do anything. As we will see a little later, this is what we see in this world today called "Humanism," that philosopy which says man is the center of all things.

David tells us in Psalm 10:4 that "the wicked will not seek God." In the first chapter of Romans we see a most hideous picture of man. Man as a race has "exchanged the truth of God for a lie, and worshiped the creature more than the Creator" (Rom. 1:25). Because of this God gave man over to his own lusts and allowed him to go his own way into destruction (vv. 28-32).

We shall come back to these thoughts, but may we see that this is the philosophy that we must not allow to permeate our own Christian lives, our Christian homes, nor our Christian churches.

B. The <u>Priorities</u> of This World System

This world system is its own religion. It worships itself. It is its own God. Therefore, the true living God is forced out and forgotten (Rom. 1:28). Therefore, anything and everything will replace any thoughts about God, everything is more important.

How tragic it is that this priority has infiltrated into many churches, and into the lives of many Christians. There are many things which are allowed to come before God. God has been forced into the back of our minds and is no longer our priority in life. We may occasionally think of religion and occasionally go to church (if it is convenient), but other than that we don't want to think about spiritual things.

A well-known text which is not often applied to Christian living is Matthew 6:33:

> But seek ye first the kingdom of God, and His righteousness, and all these things shall be added unto you.

The context of the verse speaks of Christ's instructions about prayer (vv. 9-13) and the encouragement not to lay up treasures here on the earth but to lay up treasures in heaven (vv. 19-21). This parallels Paul's teaching in Colossians 3:2:

Set your affection on things above, not on things on the earth.

But it seems like these texts mean nothing to many believers. May we ask ourselves, "What do I allow to come before God?" What do we allow to come before God's Word? Christians often allow a newspaper to take them away from reading and studying the Word of God. The same is true of our attendance in God's house. Many do not make this a priority. They allow a school activity, a job, a television program, a ballgame, or even visiting relatives to take them away from God's house. I even had a lady in one church where I was preaching say she couldn't come one night because she had to get her hair done. Again, the same is true of our service. We are so busy with other things that they take priority over being a witness for Jesus Christ.

Oh, may *nothing* come before Him!

C. The Purposes of This World System

By the purposes of this world we mean its *motives* and *methods.* The motives of the world are to glorify itself and to propagate itself. The methods it uses to do this are "whatever," anything goes. It doesn't matter who it hurts or what rules it violates.

And here again we see this has infiltrated into the lives of believers. When we serve God, do we do it to glorify God or to glorify ourselves? If we sing or play an instrument, do we do it so someone will come and compliment our talent or because we love God and do it for His glory? Do we do things in the church so the pastor will praise us or because we love the Lord?

What then are our methods? There are many today who use all sorts of gimmicks to draw people to church. They give away this thing or that thing and have this contest or that contest. They want to have a music concert, or show a film, or hear an exgangster give his testimony. However, are these "methods" of God? May we say, indeed not! I must save this discussion for another book, but we can surely see that God's Word teaches that the only thing which should be used to "draw" people to God's house is the preaching, that is, the exposition of God's Word to God's people. I think it is high time we look at all the "methods" and "programs" and so-called "ministries" we have in our churches and really compare them with the Word of God. As Paul told Timothy:

> Preach the Word; be diligent in season, out of season; reprove, rebuke, exhort with all long-suffering and doctrine (2 Tim. 4:2).

We don't need the methods, gimmicks, programs, or even the technology of the world. What we do need are preachers who exposit and apply God's Word to the lives of Christians and Christians who will *listen* to and *live* what they hear.

D. The Profits and Possessions of This World System

This point is vitally important to our present discussion for we see here the values that this world system has, and its basic value is to get more and *more* and MORE. Those of this world only want more and will usually do anything that is necessary to get it.

And, if we are to be realistic, we must agree that it is very easy for even Christians to fall into this trap because of the affluent society in which we live. However, it is nonetheless a great tragedy that many Christians today are easily fitting into the values of this world system. They just want *more.* Many are encumbered with fashion, to own a particular piece of clothing just because it has a particular designer's name or insignia on it. Many are encumbered with possessions, getting this new thing and that new thing. Many are encumbered with making a living, making as much money as possible. Many are encumbered with investments and other ways of making more money.

Dear Christian, I in no way want to preach legalistic Christianity or present a list of "do's and don'ts." What I want believers to avoid is the trap of this world system. When we fall into its trap, then the more we have the more we want, and the more we want the more we will compromise biblical standards to get it. May we not be as the rich fool in Luke 12 who said to himself, "Soul, thou has much goods laid up for many years; take thine ease. Eat, drink, and be merry." However, in verses 20 and 21, God's answer is recorded:

...thou fool, this night thy soul shall be required of thee; then whose shall those things be which thou hast provided. So is he who layeth up treasure for himself, and is not rich toward God.

Oh, may we make the verse practical which we have already quoted:

Set your affection on things above, not on things on the earth (Col. 3:2).

Does this mean earthly possessions are wrong? Of course not, as we will again touch on these things in the next chapter. However, the question is: "Where are our affections? where are our values? what do we really love and desire in life?"

E. The <u>Pleasure</u> of this World System

This follows right in line with our previous point. The world says, "Anything goes"; "If it feels good, do it." Now, of course, no real born again Christian would say that or down deep inside really believe that. However, in practical living many Christians practice this very philosophy. They practice this during those times that they follow their own desires instead of God's and do what *they* want to do instead of what *God* says to do.

Dear Christian, how often do we put our will before God's will? A verse which we will look at in more depth in the next chapter is found in James:

Therefore, to him that knoweth to do good, and doeth it not, to him it is sin (James 4:17).

We know what God's Word says and what God demands of us, but still we do not do it. *This* is sin! As we have already mentioned earlier about "priorities," we again see that many "pleasures" this world offers take many Christians away from what God desires. If there is something which takes us away from God's Word it is sin. If there is something which takes us away from God's house, it is sin. If there is something which takes us away from God's service, it is sin. We *know* what God says, so let's do it!

F. The <u>People</u> of This World System

Worldliness seeks worldliness. Worldly people seek worldly people. We must beware of our company. This is the very entreaty Paul gives us in 2 Corinthians 6:14-17. There we are instructed:

> Be ye not unequally yoked together with unbelievers . . . (v. 14).

We then see that the reason God says this is because we can't have any real "fellowship" with unbelievers. The examples Paul gives show how this is true. Righteousness has nothing in common with unrighteousness. Light has nothing in common with darkness. Christ has nothing in common with Satan. The Temple of God has nothing in common with idols.

The word "fellowship" comes from a Greek word which means, "a joint participation in a common interest and activity." To have real fellowship there must be an interest and activity in which both individuals can be involved. However, how could this be true of a Christian and a lost person? The unbeliever doesn't want the things of God and the Christian doesn't want the things of the world. How can there be fellowship?

Therefore, God says, "don't be unequally yoked." The historical background of this command is that you don't put a horse and an ox together in order to plow a field. Each one has a different walk and different pace and *can't* work together. Their very natures won't allow it. The same is true of a Christian and an unbeliever. They are not compatible. One will always have to "give in" to the will of the other and it will most always be the Christian who will need to compromise.

It is for this reason that we can say it is biblically wrong for a Christian to marry an unbeliever. It is wrong for a Christian to date an unbeliever. It is wrong for a Christian to have a business partnership with an unbeliever. It is also wrong for a Christian to be a member of a lodge or other organization with an unbelieving membership.

Why is this such a difficult principle for believers to practice these days? Many have the mistaken idea that they can pull the unbeliever up to their level; but, on the contrary, what eventually happens is the Christian is yanked down to the level of the unbeliever. It is for this reason we are told in this passage on separation:

> Wherefore, come out from among them and be ye separate saith the Lord, and touch not the unclean thing . . . (v. 17).

Let it be made very clear that we are not talking about *ostracizing* ourselves from the world, but rather we are *separating* ourselves from the world. Jesus tells us in John 17:14-18 that even though we are *in* this world we are not *of* this world. We do not separate ourselves from *contact* with the world but rather *conformity* to the world. We are in this world for one reason and that is to be a testimony of Christ.

* * * * *

These six areas we have noted are of utmost importance in laying the foundation of our study on worldliness. Where are our values? What are our priorities? Where are our affections? Are they in the world or are they in the will of God? With this foundation, let us look briefly at one other thought in this chapter.

II. A SPECIAL ILLUSTRATION OF WORLDLINESS

The illustration we need to examine has to do with the most dangerous philosophy in the history of man, the most blatant challenge to God and His revelation. Note again our earlier definition of the "world": *That order of things which is alienated from God, and in which man is the center as he opposes God and His revelation.*

Now, based upon this definition we find that there is a philosophy which has all but taken over America and the world. This philosophy is called "Secular Humanism." The definition of Secular Humanism is, "man is the measure of all things." It is a completely godless philosophy, for it says that man is the center, man is everything, and in man is every answer.

The fascinating thing to see here is that this definition of humanism (which, by the way, has been given to it by the United States Supreme Court) matches perfectly the definition of the "world." There is a *perfect* match between them. Worldliness is humanism and humanism is worldliness. The terms are synonomous and interchangeable. God chose an ancient Greek word to describe a twentieth century philosophy, though, of course, humanism has been around long before now. It is as old as man himself.

However, how does all this relate to Christians? Most Christians are totally unaware of humanism and are unaware of its effect on their lives. It is because of this that something has developed in Christians' lives and in our churches called (if I may coin the term) "Christian humanism." Simply put, this means that *we are not putting God first.*

You see, the secular humanist doesn't care about God anyway. He has nothing to do with God. He is lost. He has that picture in Romans 1 painted all over him. However, the believer who has gotten caught up with the world has fallen into "Christian humanism." He is no longer putting God first in his life, something else has replaced Him.

Now, let me say again, we are not going to make a list of "do's and don'ts." As we examine our own lives and allow the Holy Spirit to deal with us, God will then reveal to us what we are putting before Him. Let us realize that if there is anything in our everyday lives which comes before God's will, God's Word, God's house, and God's service, then it is because we have fallen into "Christian humanism." God is no longer first in our lives.

At this point I would like to present something from a historical angle. If we look at the state of America today, with its humanistic philosophy, and compare it with how the old Roman Empire fell, we see some startling and frightening parallels. As we know, the Roman Empire was never "conquered" from without but rather fell from within because of its own sin. The things which led to its collapse are frighteningly similar with what we see in America today, even in the lives of Christians. Note the historical sequence:

The *first* thing we notice is there were strong families. Rome was founded on high moral standards and each father was respected as the head of the family. In the early Republic, the father had legal authority to discipline rebellious members of his family. This matches the biblical principles of the submission of a wife and children to the spiritual leadership of the husband and father (Eph. 5:22, 6:1-4). In fact, children in the biblical times who did not obey were first beaten with the father's "rod" (or literally, a staff; Prov. 23:13), and if this did not bring submission, the rebellious child was taken out and stoned (Deut. 21:18-21). This somewhat challenges the "coddling" of young people which is going on today with "modern child psychology."

The *second* thing we see is home education. The education of the children was not the responsibility of the state but of the parents. This, therefore, strengthened the child's respect for his parents and made for a deeper family life. Again, this is a biblical teaching. The training of the children is to be done by the parents (Prov. 12:24, 19:18, 22:6, 15, 23:13-14, 29:15-17, Eph. 6:4, and so forth).

I, for one, am all for Christian schools. There is no excuse or reason for a Christian young person to be going to a public school (or more accurately, a "state school," for that is what they are). However, there is also the danger that a Christian school can turn into a substitute for what is supposed to be taught at home. We cannot deal here with this subject, but God's best is home education which, by the way, is an increasing reality these days in many Christian homes. The "second best" is the church sponsored Christian school which is not a *substitute for* the home but a *supplement to* the home.

The *third* thing we see is prosperity. Strong Roman families produced a strong nation, giving credence to that old adage: "as go the families, so goes the nation." The Roman armies were victorious in war and the wealth of conquered nations increased Roman prosperity and the standard of living.

The *fourth* thing we see is national achievements. Great building programs began in Rome. A vast network of roads united the empire. Great palaces, public buildings, and coliseums were built. It is with these last two points that we see something beginning to change, but it is with the next point that we see the crisis.

The *fifth* thing we notice is the infiltration of humanism, for as the Roman families prospered, it became fashionable to hire educated Greeks to educate the children. The philosophy of the Greeks, which was totally godless and humanistic, was passed on into Roman families. Women demanded more rights and, in order to accommodate them, new marriage contracts were designed, including "open marriages." Dear Christian, is all this beginning to sound familiar? Is this not exactly what we are seeing today? Well, let's continue, for it gets even worse.

The *sixth* thing we see is big government. By the time the first century came, the father had lost his legal authority. It was delegated first to the village, then to the city, then to the state or province, and ultimately to the empire. In Rome, citizens complained about housing shortages, high rents, congested traffic, air pollution, crime, and the high cost of living. Unemployment was a great problem, so to solve the problem, the government created a number of "civil service jobs," such as building inspectors, health inspectors, and tax collectors. Is this not frighteningly real today?

The *seventh* thing we notice is the final decline and persecution. The problems of big government only multiplied and it was these problems which finally took the Roman Empire to destruction. However, during its final years there was a flourishing New Testament church established in the Empire based upon Christ and His apostles. The final act of the Empire was to bring great persecution to Christians.

The fascinating thing to note here is that Rome was quite tolerant of all religions except Christianity. It was banned and Christians were persecuted because the very nature of Christianity is intolerant of the humanistic philosophy which is the basis of all other religions. To sum it up, by the Third Century Christianity conquered pagan Rome.

However, may we please notice that Christianity is *not* conquering pagan America, for we see today the same things which were in the Roman Empire, but we are allowing it to continue. Not only do we *allow* it, but also many Christians are even *part* of it. Many fit right into the world system of today. Many live with the same attitudes, motives, desires, priorities, values, methods, and inclinations of the humanistic world in which we live.

We must be careful at this point not to fall into the trap of "preaching on issues" as many are doing today. God tells us to "preach the Word" (2 Tim. 4:2), not to preach moral reform. When we expositorily preach the Word of God, then God will change men's hearts as they respond to His Word. The preaching of God's Word is the only thing which can do that. Men should not preach on "issues." They should preach "instruction."

However, at the same time we find Christians today who are "wishy-washy" on abortion and say there are times when it is justified. Others don't stand against "euthanasia" or, more accurately, "pulling the plug" on the sick. Still others don't see the danger in public (or state) education and don't realize that under no circumstances should a Christian young person be in a state school.

Dear Christian, we need to take a stand! This does not mean that we should stage rallies or protest marches as we have seen some do in past years. This is what the world does. However, we *do* need to take a stand. We need to stand in our homes, our churches, and our communities. When we do this and remain a testimony before the world we will see something happen as men respond to God's Word. No, maybe we can't clean up the whole world, but we can be effective in our own little corner of it. Letters to political leaders and our votes at the polls may help, but it will take God and His Word to change men's hearts.

* * * * *

I do pray that we understand what we really mean by worldliness and humanism. Many Christians are Christians by *faith*, but, sad to say, are humanistic in *practice*. That is a strong thing to say, but it is nonetheless true. May we not be caught up in religious humanism which is nothing but old fashioned worldliness. Worldliness is "enmity with God." Oh may we not have friendship with the philosophy, the priorities, the purpose, the profits and possessions, the pleasures, and the people of this "world system."

CHAPTER FIVE

The Cure
for Worldliness

In the last chapter we laid the foundation for what we mean by worldliness. I would like to conclude this subject by looking at how we can cure this worldly spirit which so easily permeates our lives. However, before we get to the *cure,* we need to look first at the *cause,* the *consequences,* and *characteristics* of worldliness as shown in James 4.

I. THE CAUSE OF WORLDLINESS

Let us note carefully James 4:1-2:

> From whence come wars and fightings among you? Come they not hence, even of your lusts that war in your members? Ye lust, and have not; ye kill, and desire to have, and cannot obtain; ye fight and war, yet ye have not because ye ask not.

We see in these two verses the central thought is that worldliness is caused by *self-will.* Please do not forget this. The root cause of worldliness is *self-will.* We have seen already how self-will ties in with the unsurrendered life, as it did in the life of King Saul (Chap. 3).

As we have also seen, this "present world system" is headed by Satan. Therefore, just as Satan fell through pride and self-will (Isa. 14:12-17), likewise did he bring into his system this very attitude of self-will and made it the very core of the system.

The Greek word that is translated "lust" in the above verse is the same word that is translated "lust" in James 1:14. This is important to understand, because in James 1:13-15 James gives us the four stages of temptation. By definition temptation is, "the urge to do evil with the promise of benefit." The first stage of temptation is *desire* (v. 14). There is nothing wrong with the natural desires of life which God has given. It is when we want to fulfill these desires outside the will of God that they become sin, that is, lust. Eating is normal, gluttony is sin. Sleep is normal; laziness is sin. Making a living is normal; greed is sin. Talking is normal; slander, gossip, lying, and foolish jesting are sin. "Marriage is honorable in all and the bed is undefiled, but whoremongers and adulterers God will judge" (Heb. 13:4).

The second stage of temptation is *deception* (v. 14). No temptation looks like temptation. There is always "the promise of benefit." The word "enticed" means "to bait a hook." Temptation always carries with it something that appeals to the natural desire, but this "bait" hides the consequences just as the worm hides the fisherman's hook. Please ponder this: *It is better to shun the bait than to struggle in the snare,* for as Numbers 32:23 tells us, "Be sure your sin will find you out."

The third stage of temptation is *disobedience* (v. 15). When there is a fleshly desire and a deception of the mind, this then gives birth to the disobedience of the will. Christian living is a matter of the will and the intellect, not the emotions. The reason so many Christians yield to temptation is that they allow the emotions, that is, their desires, to rule their lives.

The fourth stage of temptation is *death* (v. 15). God's warning is plain, "Be sure your sin will find you out." Look at Eve, Achan, Lot, David, and so many others. Sin, when it is finished, brings death. We say again, "It is better to shun the bait than to struggle in the snare."

We make all this clear so we may understand the use of

"lust" in James 4:1-2. The word is again showing the fulfilling of the natural desires of life outside the will of God. Therefore, it is self-will. Note the emphasis on self in these verses: "*your* lusts," "*your* members," "*you* fight," "*you* war." The emphasis is totally on self and upon *our* will, not *God's* will.

As we draw this chapter to a close we will come back to the thrust in this book about total dedication and surrender of the will, for without a surrender of the will, there will be nothing but worldliness. This is the direct parallel to Romans 12:1-2, because our presentation *must* come before our separation.

So, the cause of worldliness in the Christian's life is self-will. Our self-will is evident no matter what the situation. James tells us later in his letter that self-will is evident whether it is the desire for possessions and money or whether it is arguments with other Christians. At the root of it all is *self-will* and it is this that *must* be conquered by the Spirit of God. Just as the will of a child must be conquered before he can ever be controlled, so must the will of a believer be conquered before God can ever work with him.

Verse 2 reads, "ye have not because ye ask not." In essence James is saying, "You think you can do it on your own. You are the one who is striving, and the reason you don't have God's provision is because you don't ask for it." Oh, how much of this self-striving we have today! Men and women today, many of them Christians, are striving for more money, possessions, and success.

We talk a lot about pornography today and how bad it is. Indeed, it is bad! However, the second worst literature is the "self-improvement" section in secular bookstores. You can go there and pick up books on self-motivation, self-success, and self-assertiveness. Many Christians are reading these and listening to speakers talk about it and are "sucked in" to believing that "I can be successful and bring glory to God." However, may we ask ourselves, "Is that God's will? Does God want me successful in the eyes of the world?" The world defines success differently than God does. The world looks at *pleasure, possessions,* and *popularity,* as John tells us in 1 John 2:16. God says success is doing His will.

How important all this is! For self-will is the cause of most, if not *all* our sin. And just as *self-will* is the *root-cause* of worldliness, we will see later that *submission* is the *root of the cure.*

II. THE CONSEQUENCES OF WORLDLINESS

In verses 3-6 James presents two basic consequences of worldliness. The *first* consequence is "a completely defeated prayer life and, therefore, a completely defeated spiritual life." Note verse 3:

> Ye ask, and receive not, because ye ask amiss, that ye may consume it upon your lusts.

What we see here is that the first consequence of wanting what this world has is total defeat, total despair, a total lack of peace, and a total lack of joy.

In Chapter 10 of this book we will study "prayer" and will contrast it with "prayers." However, basically stated "prayer" is "a constant communion with God," an every moment consciousness of Him and His presence. "Prayers" are those specific times when we bring our praises, thanksgivings, confessions, intercessions, and petitions to God.

Therefore, the first consequence of worldliness is a defeated spiritual life because of a defeated prayer life. Worldliness cuts off our communion, our fellowship with God. The first theological truth we all learn about sin is, "sin separates." As we saw in the last chapter, those who have a tender affection for this world are at enmity with God.

Notice again verse 2–"Ye have not because ye ask not." James is saying, "You don't pray. You're not in communion. You're not walking with God. You don't have because you don't ask. You lean upon yourself instead of leaning upon God."

However, note verse 3 once again. When you *do* pray you still don't get what you pray for. The reason is because you ask "amiss," that is, you ask with the wrong motive. How often do you pray and pray for something and don't get it? It could very well be because you ask for the wrong reason. It could be because you want it for yourself, to use it for yourself. Oh, how often we want things we don't need and need things that we don't want! Every time we pray for something we must ask ourselves, "Why am I praying for this? Is it something that is going to glorify God or is it going to be used for myself?" There is nothing wrong with desires, but those desires must match God's desires.

The *second* consequence of worldliness is akin to the first. It is "an alienation from God." We have continually emphasized verse 4 in our study of worldliness because of its plain statement of the enmity between God and this world. "Ye adulterers and adulteresses, know ye not that the friendship of the world is enmity with God? Whosoever, therefore, will be a friend of the world is the enemy of God." This one thing should deeply frighten us into realizing the seriousness of worldliness. A worldly attitude cuts us off from God.

It is tragic to think of that marvelous truth that Jesus has "broken down the middle wall of partition" between us and God (Eph. 2:14) only to see us "rebuild it" because of worldliness. We are the ones who willfully cut ourselves off from God.

Many Christians today live a "mechanical" life and a defeated life but don't know why. One day is just like every other day. They get up, go to work, come home, say "hi" to the family, read the newspaper, eat dinner, watch television, go to sleep, and get up and do it all over again. There's something missing. Everyday they work, and sweat, and fret, but still there is a void. The reason for this is because they are caught up in the world system. They are allowing the world to dictate every aspect of their lives and they will not stand up and say "No!" to the world.

The parallel to this is found in the history of the Jews. They were called "adulterers and adulteresses," just as James is doing now because they had mingled with the world. A marvelous Old Testament type! God told His people to keep themselves unspotted from the Gentiles around them. However, when they intermingled and intermarried with the world, God judged them for it. God will likewise judge New Testament believers when they mingle with the world! Again, as we saw in the last chapter, Paul's command was "be not unequally yoked" (2 Cor. 6:14-18). It was true *then* and it is true *now.*

Oh, dear Christian, we will be alienated from God because of worldliness. Our Christian lives will suffer, our homes will suffer, our churches will suffer, and the entire Body of our

Saviour will suffer. Oh, the consequences of worldliness.

How often are we, just as the Israelites, not only "adultress," but "idolatrous" as well? We do not want to make a list, but may we rather look at ourselves and see what is an idol in our lives. Oh, how often we put the things of this world before the things of God and "worship the creature more than the Creator" (Rom. 1:25).

III. THE CHARACTERISTICS OF WORLDLINESS

In verses 11-17 we find there are three major things which, when present in our lives, reveal an inward attitude of worldliness.

A. Speaking Against Fellow Christians

Verses 11 and 12 are very challenging. The first characteristic of worldliness is speaking against another Christian. Is it not instructive that this is the first characteristic? We don't often think of gossip, backbiting, and cutting humor, as worldliness. However, on the contrary, it heads the list of worldly behavior.

This is the subject James deals with in Chapter 3. He points out that like a fire, the tongue is capable of incredible destruction (vv. 5-6). He shows also that it is full of deadly poison and that it is impossible to control (v. 7). He continues in the chapter to paint a horrible picture of what an unruly tongue can do.

Likewise, in Proverbs 6:16-19 there is a list of seven things which are an abomination to God. They are "a proud look, a *lying tongue,* hands that shed innocent blood, a heart that deviseth wicked imagination, feet that are swift in running to mischief, *a false witness that speaketh lies,* and *he that soweth discord among the brethren."* I emphasized the three out of the seven which are sins of the tongue.

All of this is most important, for here in James 4 we are told that all of this stems from worldliness, it stems from self-will. Think of all this. Why do we have arguments, strifes, divisions, and all sorts of problems in our churches? Why do preachers today tear one another down in print and from the pulpit? The answer is self-will. We want everything our way. This is the reason for the disunity in the Body of Christ today. One denomination can't get along with another denomination. One church can't get along with another church. One preacher can't get along with another preacher. One school can't get along with another school. And none of these will get along with anyone who does get along with someone whom they don't get along. Did you get that?

Now, what James is telling us here is that speaking against a fellow Christian (whether in person, in print, or in the pulpit) is worldly. It is nothing but self-will and an identification with the devil and his system, for one of his greatest desires is to see us fighting among ourselves. When we speak against a fellow brother or sister in Christ, we immediately alienate ourselves from God.

Constantly the Apostle Paul spoke of unity (Eph. 4, Phil. 2:4; 1 Cor. 3). We will not always agree on every *detail*, but let us all have the same *desire*. That is, to increase and strengthen the Body of Christ. We will not always agree on "the minors" but let us agree on "the majors." Oh, how we need unity! I did not say compromise, I said unity. Let us stop having divided Christians, divided churches and divided schools. More than anything else, let us *stop* dividing and splitting the Body of Christ into countless pieces!

Dear Christian, be careful of the things you say. How tragic it is that many love *gossip* instead of *godliness.* How tragic it is that we have many *slanderers* but few *students* of God's Word. How disgraceful it is that we have many *busybodies* and few *bearers* of God's truth. Many Christians who seem to be the most spiritual Christians in the church are the ones with the loosest tongues. It is vital that we give our tongues over to divine control. When Christ is Lord of our *lives*, He will also be the Lord of our *lips.*

B. A Desire for Material Wealth

Verses 13-17 tells us of this second characteristic of worldliness. Charles Ryrie in his *Ryrie Study Bible* gives an explanation of this passage. He says, "The folly of forgetting God in business is another manifestation of worldliness. The itinerant merchants addressed here were Jews who carried on a lucrative trade throughout the world." The main point to ponder is that they forgot God in financial matters. They were saying, "*we* are going to go and *we* are going to increase."

However, let us notice how they got their money in Chapter 5. They first of all held back the wages of their employees (v. 4). They also, according to verse 6, as well as historical evidence, controlled the court system of the day.

We then notice how they used their money. They hoarded it, they stored it up, and they invested it only so they could get more for themselves (v. 3). They also kept others from benefiting from it and withheld it from those who deserved to share it (v. 4). Lastly, they lived in luxury and cared only for their own comfort (v. 5).

Let it be clear in our minds that James is writing to Christians! He is writing to Christians who were caught up in the philosophy of the world that says, "all that matters is to get material wealth." *This* is the attitude of the world. This was the attitude of the rich fool in Luke 12. This is the attitude of many Christians today.

At this point in our study I would like for us to ponder what our relationship as Christians should be to money and material possessions. We hear much about these things. What should our attitude be toward all this? Let us look at three basic principles.

1. These things must not be an end in themselves. Many believers today think that God gave them a job so they could "make a living" or so they could provide for their needs. However, this is the wrong attitude. Paul tells us in Ephesians 4:28:

> Let him who stole steal no more, but, rather let him labour, working with his hands the thing which is good, that he may have to give to him that needeth.

The reason God gives us a job is not so we can store up money, not so we can get all the things we want, but rather our motive is that we may give to those in need. Yes, this includes our family, but it also includes the church and His service. Many work in order to *get,* but God says we work in order to *give.*

It is quite possible that the best thing that could happen to many Christians is to lose their job. Maybe they would then realize that *they* are not the ones who provide their needs but it is *God* who provides their needs. This is the whole point of Philippians 4:19:

But my God shall supply all your need according to His riches in glory by Christ Jesus.

But may we also note the context of the verse (vv. 14-19). This verse is *not* an unconditional promise. Paul is thanking the Philippian believers for their sacrificial giving to his needs. It is after this commendation that Paul tells them God will supply. We see from this that if we are not using money as God desires, He then will not supply.

This parallels James' teaching "ye have not because ye ask not." If we live in our own self-sufficiency and don't claim God's provision, then He will not supply. We must be good stewards of God's money, use it wisely, and give it sacrificially. Our attitude must be that money and material things are not our goal.

There are indeed some dangerous practices in Christianity today. One of them is "overtime." Working overtime is not in itself sinful, but often people want overtime just so they can get more money to use for themselves. Often the time men spent working overtime could be better invested in spending more time with their family and with the Lord.

Another thing which is being practiced by Christians today, and which is a most sinful and disgraceful practice, is that of working on Sunday. Many Christians think nothing at all of forsaking God's house because some ungodly employer says, "You have to work on Sunday." Oh, to have Christians with enough courage to say, "No, I don't." Many say, "If I don't work, I'll get fired." Personally I have known many Christians who have taken a stand in this area and not one of them has lost his job. But, even if they did, God would supply their needs and give them another job according to His will. We will come back to this subject in a later chapter on faithfulness (Chap. 7). However, the emphasis of our study on worldliness is that we not allow the world to dictate what our standards of conduct and values are going to be.

Another dangerous practice today is working wives and mothers. Many are convinced that if the wife does not work, then the family can't make it. However, the fact which is usually true is that they can't live like *they want* to live, but they could live the way *God wants* them to live. However, the most important fact remains that the Scriptures teach that the place of the wife is in the home. Paul told Titus that the older women of the church were to teach the younger woman. Titus 2:4-5 reads:

> That they may teach the young women to be sober-minded, to love their husbands, to love their children, to be discreet, chaste, keepers at home, good, obedient to their own husbands, that the Word of God be not blasphemed.

These are strong words in this day and age, but they are God's words, and His words must not be ignored nor explained away by our excuses. Equally instructive is that well-known portrait of a virtuous woman in Proverbs 31. The entire passage speaks of the concern of the wife for the home. When we ponder verses 13, 15, 19, 21, and 27, we can come to no other conclusion. I know this teaching is not popular today, but, then, neither is God's Word. I will leave further study of this to a future book. But I would strongly urge every Christian to read "The Family," an excellent book by Dr. John MacArthur.

Another dangerous practice today is that teen-agers are allowed to work too much at a secular job. While it is fine that we teach them "money management," it is equally important that we teach them the right values. The average working teen-ager works to make money for himself, thereby setting the stage for values he will keep for the rest of his life. Many have the mistaken idea that the most important thing we can teach our children is "how to make a living." This is totally false! The most important thing we can teach our children is to love God and put Him first in their lives. All other matters of life will then begin to fall into place.

We mention all these dangers simply because they are being used to blind Christians with the philosophy that all that matters is what you have materially—the biggest house, the biggest car, the number of cars, the furniture, the expensive "play things" and all the rest. The world says if you don't have all this, you will not be happy. Howard Hughes, one of the richest men who ever lived, died a lonely and unhappy man. Money and possessions will leave you empty.

I am always burdened for Christians when I think of Martha in Luke 10:38-42. Martha's sister, Mary, sat and listened to Jesus while Martha did all the serving. She then complained and asked Jesus to tell Mary to help her serve. The words of Jesus are loving but also admonishing:

> ...Martha, Martha, thou art anxious and troubled about many things. But one thing is needful, and Mary hath chosen that good part, which shall not be taken away from her.

She was so encumbered with temporal things that she missed the presence of Jesus. I fear this to be the case in the lives of many Christians today.

It is shocking at how some Christians treat worldliness. There are some today called "prosperity teachers" who teach that material prosperity glorifies God and shows His blessing on a person; whereas poverty is a curse. These teachers say that God desires "above all things that you may prosper" (3 John 2). We are "King's Kids" (what an irreverent term!); and if we are not prospering financially, then Satan is robbing us of our inheritance in Christ. They say the secret to prosperity is "give and it shall be given unto you" (Luke 6:38). If you give to the Lord, He promises you a hundredfold return in this life (Mark 10:30). Invest in God, and be prosperous for His glory!

This is disgusting, not to mention ungodly, and leads us right into our second basic principle.

2. Are we investing in heaven or in the earth? Once again may we meditate upon Colossians 3:2:

> Set your affection on things above, not on things on the earth.

With this verse firmly set in our hearts, let us then look at Matthew 6:19-24 and 33:

> Lay not up for yourselves treasures upon earth ... but lay up for yourselves treasures in heaven ... for where your treasure is there will your heart be also. No man can serve two masters; for either he will hate the one and love the other; or else he will hold to the one, and despise the other. Ye cannot serve God and money.
> . . .
> But seek ye first the kingdom of God and His righteousness, and all these things shall be added unto you.

Now, how do those "prosperity teachers" deal with this? This passage follows Jesus' teaching on prayer and fasting (vv. 6-18) and how *He* will provide our *daily* needs "according to His riches in glory" (Phil. 4:19).

As for the "proof texts" that these teachers give, we need

only point out that the context of Mark 10:30 shows that when we leave behind all the world has to offer, God will then prosper us, not in material things, but rather in God's attitude of prosperity, which is, He will supply our *needs.*

Dear Christian, where are our treasures? Many Christians have been convinced by the world that you have to have all sorts of investments. They think they need this stock, that bond, this certificate, that account, and all sorts of other securities. I even know preachers who advocate this sort of thing for they have investments in diamonds and gold. On top of all this, many Christians are "insurance poor" and trust insurance companies instead of God.

The point is this, everything of this nature is from *the world's* viewpoint. Please think about it! The world says you have to take care of yourself. God says He will take care of you. The question is, in whom are we trusting?

There are those who would use the parable of the talents (Matt. 25:14-30), the parable of the unjust steward (Luke 16:1-10) and the parable of the long journey (Luke 19:11-27) to teach investing and getting gain. Space does not allow a full study of this, but may we submit that this teaching does not match the Scriptures we have already seen. These parables teach us to use what God has given us in order to glorify him, not increase ourselves.

In what are we investing? Are we investing in the things on this earth or in the things of heaven? Are we concerned with how to "make it" here, or are we concerned with what we are accomplishing for eternity? We are often so busy with a job and all the other temporal matters that our spiritual lives and spiritual values are left behind; no rewards in heaven, no crowns awaiting, no one we have been a witness to, no personal spiritual growth. Oh, in what are we investing?

3. Buying is not synonymous with borrowing. This last principle is not thought about very much these days. I shall never forget one church I was in some years ago. I pulled up in front of this large, brandnew building and saw its beauty. I then went inside and saw the chandeliers, padded pews, wall-to-wall carpet, modern P.A. system, large sanctuary, and all the additional adornments. Then I remembered the sign in the church yard which gave the church name and the statement, "Built to

the glory of God." I shall never forget that I wondered how much money those believers borrowed to build that building to "the glory of God." I later found out that they were in debt $200,000 for that building.

This is the philosophy of the world, *borrow*. But God's philosophy is to *trust*. Many churches fall into this trap. They say we will borrow the money and then trust the Lord to give us the payments instead of allowing God to provide in the first place. When we truly *need* something, God will then supply it and not before. We don't need the world's money to build God's work. I have seen many churches and Christian institutions destroyed because they would not lean on God. Likewise, Christians, in their personal finances, need to realize that they can get along with a lot less and should not shackle themselves in the bondage of debt.

I have not given these three principles to "meddle," but rather I gave them to present the attitude of keeping our eyes on the right priorities and values in this life, to keep our eyes on God and His Word and prepare ourselves and others for eternity. When God saved us, He did not leave us here to *get more* but rather *to be less*, that He may increase while we decrease. Money and material things are neither right nor wrong, but the question is, "What do we really want from life?"

C. Disregard for God's Will

There is one last characteristic which by now seems quite obvious. In James, verses 13-17, we see a complete disregard for the will of God! This point is really the focal point of this book, God's will apart from our will.

The problem the believers had here in James was that they were saying "this is what we're going to do." But verse 15 is the key:

> For ye ought to say, if the Lord will, we shall live, and do this, or that.

This *must* be how we live. If it is God's will, we will get up tomorrow morning. If it is God's will, we will go to work. If it is God's will we'll stay healthy. If it is God's will, we will have certain possessions. We must note verse 17 very carefully:

> Therefore, to him that knoweth to do good, and doeth it not, to him it is sin.

We can only understand this verse fully when we take it in the context. What *is* God telling us to do? What do we know to be good? The context tells us that God says live according to His will, don't live according to self-will, and don't be encumbered with this world. We *know* what God says and if we do not obey, it is sin. That very sin cuts us off from God.

We'll come back to this thought of disregarding God's will as we close this chapter.

III. THE CURE FOR WORLDLINESS

We come now to how we can cure this attitude of worldliness in our lives. Space does not permit a deep study, but there are ten verbs in verses 7 to 10. All of these verbs are in a tense which indicates a decisive and urgent break with the world. As we study this passage, we find there are three basic thoughts James presents which will cure this attitude of worldliness. They are presented in order and are tied together. We must have them all or we will continue in worldliness.

A. Submit to God

Note verse 7:

> Submit yourselves, therefore, to God. Resist the devil, and he will flee from you.

Here is a direct parallel to the main text of this book, Romans 12:1-2. We *cannot* know "separation" until first there has been a "presentation." The first step in victory over this world system is a total, complete, unconditional surrender to the will of God. The word "submit" comes from a word in the Greek which means "to subordinate; to bring under influence" and again is in that once-for-all aorist tense. Submitting ourselves to God's will is the only way we are going to be able to *reject* the world, *rebuke* the flesh, and *resist* the devil.

B. Draw Near to God

Verse 8 reads:

> Draw near to God and He will draw near to you. Cleanse your hands, ye sinners; and purify your hearts, ye double minded.

Note that this verse puts the responsibility on *us* to draw near to God. Why? Because His presence is with us. We are the ones who forsake *Him* and go to the world. He demands that we cleanse our *hands* of the world's possessions and purify our *hearts* and minds of the world's attitudes.

He says, "Draw near." This again parallels Romans 12:1-2, for it speaks of our "transformation," our prayer, our meditation, our study of His Word and our communion with Him.

The word "double minded" carries the idea of "divided allegiance" and James also used it in Chapter 1, verse 8. All this ties in with what we have seen in this chapter. We *can't* love God *and* the world. They do not mix. In order to draw near to God, we have to get farther away from the world.

C. Humble Ourselves to God

James also says in Chapter 4, verse 9 and 10:

> Be afflicted, and mourn, and weep; let your laughter be turned to mourning, and your joy to heaviness. Humble yourselves in the sight of the Lord and He shall lift you up.

At first glance we might think humbling ourselves is the same as submitting ourselves. However, in reality, this humbling is a continuation of the "submission" and the "drawing near." Verse 9 shows the seriousness of worldliness and shows us that we should be truly broken-hearted at the thought of it. May we continually live in an attitude of sobriety and seriousness from self and the world. We *must* be on guard each moment we live.

* * * * *

Beloved Christian, the things in this chapter (and the last chapter) are not easy to live, and, please, believe me, they are not any easier for me to live, or even say. However, they are what God has laid on my own heart about this world system. It has crept into *every* area of our lives and God is trying to tell us that if we are friends with it, then we are at enmity with Him.

PART III

MORE
ABOUT
TRANSFORMATION

CHAPTER SIX

"Grow in Grace and Knowledge

There are two Scripture references which are indeed inseparable:

> But grow in grace and in the knowledge of our Lord and Saviour Jesus Christ . . . (2 Peter 3:18).

> But the fruit of the Spirit is love, joy, peace, long-suffering, gentleness, goodness, faith, meekness, self-control, against such there is no law (Gal. 5:22-23).

The reason these verses are inseparable is because we are instructed to "grow in Christ." The tense of the verb "grow" is the present imperative, that is, a *command* to be *continually* growing in grace and knowledge. A literal translation would be "keep on growing in Christ!" This is a most important principle to the Christian. We are instructed to continuously grow day-by-day in Christ.

What we want to examine is what it means to "grow in *grace* and *knowledge.*"

I. GROW IN GRACE

What does it mean to "grow in grace"? What we must see first is that God's grace has been given equally to every man. The simple, basic definition of "grace" is *unmerited favor.* This favor has been given by God to every man. No man has more than another. Therefore, to "grow in grace" does not mean we *get* more grace but that we *grow* in the grace already in our possession.

G. Campbell Morgan put it this way, "Being in grace, we grow in answer to it: we develop in response to it." We are manifesting, radiating, growing, developing, and responding to the grace we possess. However, some might ask, "What about James, Chapter 4, verse 6, 'He giveth more grace'?" The word there for "more" is the word *megas* where we get the English prefix "mega." It means "great; large in size" and can also be translated "splendid, magnificent, extraordinary, or wonderful." As the remainder of the verse tells us, this great grace can only be manifested when we are humble. God's grace is indeed great!

To put it simply, *to grow in grace is to become more like Christ.* There are those who say, "It's not possible to be more like Christ. We can never be exactly like Him so there is no sense in trying." We cannot agree with this. Here in Galatians 5:22 and 23 are the characteristics of grace. These are the things God is trying to produce in our lives. God wants these characteristics of *Christ* to be the characteristics of *Christians.* And through the Holy Spirit we can indeed be more like Christ.

To emphasize this we need to look very carefully at that phrase, "the fruit of the Spirit." It does *not* say "fruits," it says "fruit" (singular). Many have the mistaken idea that these are "fruits" we go out and pick from the "spiritual orchard." This makes it sound like we can have one or two of the "fruits" and be okay, or as long as we've got maybe six out of the nine, then we are growing in grace. Wrong! The "fruit of the Spirit" are these *nine Christian graces.* Please get this, they must *all* be present in our lives before we are manifesting the Spirit of God in our lives and showing Christ-likeness. These are the qualities the Holy Spirit is trying to produce in us which show we are becoming more like Christ.

It's not enough for us to have just love, joy, and peace. We must have the others to see and know the Holy Spirit's control in our lives. Only when we possess and practice all nine "graces" will we truly grow, reproduce, and abound in the Lord.

We must also realize that it is not *we* who are striving to produce these *graces,* it is not through our effort that they will be possessed. It is only through the Holy Spirit's working in us that these *graces* will be produced. We are not to be consciously working on each *grace* but rather "walking in the Spirit" (Gal. 5:16) and allowing *Him* to produce them. I urge the reader to read *He That Is Spiritual* by Lewis Sperry Chafer as his insights are most valuable.

In the same way many today speak of the "spiritual gifts" and they urge Christians to follow certain rules to "find their spiritual gift." This is not scriptural. God does not want us to *seek* the gifts, He wants us to *receive* them. When we are totally dedicated to Christ, and when the Holy Spirit has control, we will then receive the gifts that God wants us to use.

The way we grow in grace is revealed to us in these two verses and I want to break them down not only into the nine "graces" themselves, but I also want to show the natural division of the nine into three district categories.

A. Personal

The first three Christian graces (love, joy, peace) are *personal.* That is, they are the true basis of our growth in Christ and are the basis for all the others. They come about *only* by a personal experience of Christ and are absolutely unique to Christianity. May we not forget this uniqueness. No other "religion" nor faith can profess these three personal Christian graces. They are just that. Personal! And beyond measure. They are the true basis and foundation for all that happens in the Christian life.

1. *Love*—The first Christian grace is love and pouring out of it are all the rest. Without this love nothing else is possible. The same love God showed to us through the death, burial, and resurrection of Jesus Christ is the same as the love He now wants us to show in our daily walk with Christ.

The love spoken of here is not the Greek *philos* which means "a tender affection," but is the word *agape* which is "a divine, selfless, all-giving love which gives itself totally to the recipient." May we ask ourselves, "How much do we really love the Lord Jesus?"

As I mentioned in Chapter 2, one of my favorite passages is Philippians 3:10: "That I may know Him and the power of His resurrection . . . ." In the context (vv. 7-10), Paul said that he was willing to give up everything in the world for Jesus Christ because he loved Him and wanted to know Him in a *personal, progressive,* and *powerful* way.

Space does not allow a full treatment of this but we are told in that context that Paul was willing to do three things in order to know Christ better. First, he was willing to *sacrifice* everything he had and consider everything as worthless "refuse" that he might know Christ more. Second, he was willing to *suffer* for the cause of Christ that he might know Him more. And, third, Paul said he was willing to *surrender* himself totally to Christ in order to know Him more.

Dear Christian, how much do you really love the Lord? We quite often say we love Him, but do we *really love* Him? Is He everything to you? Is His Word the most important possession you have? You will find that how much you love the Lord will dictate everything else in your life. The first "Christian grace" we all must have is love—love for Him and then love for those around us.

2. *Joy*—The second "grace" is joy and, oh, what joy we have in Christ! I do wish we could spend a chapter's worth of time on this one word, but we can't. But do we *really* have joy in the Christian life? By joy we do not mean that relative state called "happiness" for happiness is something which just comes and goes. By joy we mean that absolute, definite state of spiritual gladness; a gladness for what Jesus has done. No matter what the circumstances may be, we know that real joy is in Christ.

One of my favorite authors and preachers is Dr. J. Sidlow Baxter. I heard him some years ago give a very practical contrast between joy and happiness: "When happenings happen to happen happily you have happiness; but when happenings happen to happen unhappily you have unhappiness; so, happiness is nothing more than circumstancial happenness; but joy is completely independent of circumstances."

What a marvelous contrast, and we know that the only way

true joy comes is by the infilling and controlling of the Holy Spirit. True joy is the opposite of despondency, depression, anxiety, and even indifference. Spiritual joy is the absolute spiritual gladness which we have in Christ. It's not based on circumstances. It is based on what we have in Him and that is what makes the difference. Aren't you glad that it does not depend on us but upon the absoluteness of Christ?

I've heard it said that "True joy is a mountain spring; always refreshing, overflowing with praise." This matches that principle in James 1:2: "Count it all joy when you fall into various trials." This verse does not mean we are going to be "happy" and feel good in times of sickness or tragedy, but it *is* telling us that we as Christians look at these things in a different light. The word "count" means consider or evaluate. When sickness, accident, disappointment, death, or other tragedy comes, *we evaluate it in the light of what God is doing in us and through us.* He allows these things to come to bring out the best in us. God is constantly developing us and it is through difficulties that we grow.

This principle is not *emotionalism* but it is true *enthusiasm.* It is tragic indeed that the world has perverted that term enthusiasm. Many lost people in the sales world today talk about being "enthusiastic" about their product not knowing what the word means. The word comes from two Greek words. The first is *en* meaning "within" and the second is *theos* meaning "God." Therefore, true enthusiasm is "God within." No one who is lost can know real enthusiasm. They may be excited or emotional but they can't be enthused.

Only a Christian can know joy:

> For the kingdom of God is not food and drink, but righteousness, and peace, and joy in the Holy Spirit (Rom. 14:17).

> And having this confidence, I know that I shall abide and continue with you all for your furtherance and joy of faith (Phil. 1:25).

> Rejoice in the Lord (Phil. 2:1, 4:4).

> And these things write we unto you, that your joy may be full (1 John 1:4).

Oh, the joy we have in Him!

3. *Peace*—The third personal grace is peace. There are four aspects of peace spoken of in the New Testament. The first is

"Peace *with* God" spoken of in Romans 5:1, "Being justified by faith, we have peace with God, through our Lord Jesus Christ." This peace shows us that we are no longer at enmity, that is, at war with God. There is no longer that barrier of sin between God and man. When Christ is accepted as Saviour we then have peace with God. However, then as a Christian we possess another aspect of peace, "Peace *of* God." We are told in Philippians 4:6-7, "the peace of God, which passeth all understanding, shall keep your hearts and minds through Christ Jesus." As believers we not only have peace with God, but we also have a constant and continuing "peace of mind" because of this marvelous peace *of* God. This is an inward peace, a peace that only Christians can know because they have peace *with* God, and a peace that conquers all anxiety and worry through prayer and meditation on God's Word.

Another aspect of peace is "Peace *from* God" which is used constantly in the salutations of Paul's epistles (Rom. 1:7, 1 Cor. 1:3, and so forth). This reference to peace shows us from where all *true* peace comes. The world *talks* about peace, but God *transfers* peace from Himself to believers. Outside of Christ there is no peace. The last aspect of peace is "Peace on earth" which refers to the universal peace that will be present on the earth during the millennial reign of Christ (Psa. 72:7. 75:10; Isa. 9:6-7, 11:1-12).

Christian, do you lack peace? Is there a void in your life? Do you have real peace in your heart that you're doing what God wants you to do and are where God wants you to be?

B. Social

The next three "Christian graces" are social in natuıe. While the first three are personal, the next three are social, for they illustrate that command of Jesus "Love thy neighbor as thyself." These three social graces show how we should appear to society, that is, how we must deal with those around us, both saved and unsaved.

1. *Patience*—The first social grace is long-suffering or patience. The Greek word used here is *makrothumia; makro* meaning long and *thumia* meaning temper. Putting these together, we see we are to "suffer long" and have a "long temper," which is, of course, the opposite of a "short temper." This is the attitude of

bearing injury or injustice without revenge and this is how we are to act to society. This is the way we are to appear to those around us. What a marvelous testimony it is to be long-suffering, to be patient, to have the ability to be long-tempered. "Love suffers long" (1 Cor. 13:4) and we must be "swift to hear, slow to speak, and slow to wrath" (James 1:19).

When we are impatient with people and when we are short-tempered, it is really because we are impatient with God. We are at that moment not trusting and not leaning upon Him to give us strength. A verse which is not quoted enough and lived consistently by Christians is Isaiah 40:31:

> But they that wait upon the Lord shall renew their strength; they shall mount up with wings like eagles; they shall run and not be weary; and they shall walk and not faint.

When we wait upon God and allow Him to rule in our lives, and let Him "right the wrongs" that people do to us, then He renews our strength in three stages: a) During the easy times we will soar like eagles. It's quite easy to live for the Lord when all goes well, but it is also during these times that we must lean upon *Him* lest we become puffed-up; b) Then during the everyday difficulties of life we may not soar as eagles but we will still run and not grow tired if we are leaning on Him; c) And then during the serious problems and tragedies we will still be able to walk along without collapsing if we lean on Jesus.

There is a great challenge here for us as believers to be patient. What a testimony it is to those around us when we can wait upon the Lord and manifest Him in our lives. This social grace comes only by allowing the Holy Spirit to produce it in us.

2. *Kindness*—The second social grace is kindness or, as it is in the King James Version, "gentleness." The Greek word used here, however, is best translated "kindness." It is a word which is used only in the writings of the Apostle Paul throughout the New Testament. He used it for example in 2 Corinthians 6:6 where kindness is one of the many characteristics of the true Christian worker.

This kindness means a serene, loving, sympathizing temperament. It is that "soft answer that turns away wrath (Prov. 25:1). This is one thing that Christianity as a whole is lacking today. It is difficult to manifest an attitude of kindness in every situation, but it is vital that we allow the Holy Spirit to produce this Christ-like characteristic in us. "Be ye kind one to another, tenderhearted, forgiving one another, even as God, for Christ's sake has forgiven you" (Eph. 4:32).

3. *Goodness*—We now come to the third social grace, that of goodness. The meaning of this goodness is "uprightness and morality." Paul uses this word again in Ephesians 5:9: "For the fruit of the Spirit is in all goodness, righteousness, and truth." One of the great needs of America and the world is morality, but the only place they are going to see it manifested is in the Christian. This principle of goodness must balance the previous principle of kindness. We must not be so kind that we allow immorality, but as we deal with immorality may we do it with kindness.

It is tragic indeed that many Christians often talk, act, think, and look like the world. It is even more tragic when some of them say "Well, this is necessary so that we may identify with the lost so we can win them to Christ." Other Christians don't manifest morality because of laziness, fear, or just indifference. However, whatever *excuse* we use, the *reason* is still the same— we do not have the courage and character of Christ to stand against immorality and live holy.

Oh, how important it is to have a holy life. In later chapters we will examine more of the Scripture teaching on holiness and living apart from worldliness, but may we grasp this truth, that as we live in this society we *must* manifest holiness.

C. Philosophical

The last three Christian graces are philosophical, that is, they are given to show the basic contrast between the attitudes of God and the attitudes of the world. These three philosophical graces are the exact opposites of the world's philosophies.

1. *Faithfulness*—The first basic philsophy we must have is faithfulness. The Greek word here is *pistos* which does not mean "faith" but "faithfulness." It is the same word used in 1 Corinthians 4:2 which we will examine closely in a separate chapter on faithfulness. However, simply put, our faithfulness is our reliability, our trustworthiness, our consistency. This is something the world doesn't want. They want to do what they want to do. Man doesn't by nature want to be responsible.

How tragic it is that this lack of faithfulness has crept into our churches, our homes, and our lives. So many believers today think, act, and even have the same priorities and values that the world has, and are no longer trustworthy and faithful to God.

That is why this grace is "philosophical." The word philosophy is not a bad word. What is right or wrong is what the philosophy *is*. Everyone has a philosophy or "attitude of life." The first basic godly attitude of life is faithfulness. God wants believers who He can count on, those who are trustworthy, reliable, and consistent.

2. *Meekness*—The second underlying philosophy we must have is meekness. It has been truthfully stated many times that "meekness is not weakness, but strength under control." The best illustration of real meekness is the Lord Jesus. One of my favorite songs records:

He could have called ten thousand angels,
To destroy the world, and set Him free;
He could have called ten thousand angels,
But he died alone for you and me.

Our Saviour had the power of the universe at His command. Is that not strength? However, still the Scriptures say He was meek. In addition to this our Saviour was strong physically. The liberals and the world would have us believe Jesus was weak and even effeminate, but could a weakling carry a timber weighing as much as 150-200 pounds? Jesus did! (see John 19:17). However, even with all that strength, Jesus was meek, for His strength was under control.

Here again is something the world knows nothing about. Man knows a lot about power, a lot about strength, but nothing about meekness and humility. Man thinks he's so far advanced. He can even reach out into space, split the atom, and computerize almost anything. However, he shakes his fist in the face of God and says "We have power and control. We don't need a God." Then a hurricane comes along and devastates an entire shoreline and man finds out just how weak he really is.

Meekness is strength and power under control. It is the opposite of self-interest, self-assertiveness, and self-direction. What is needed today are Christians who are meek and humble, Christians who know the power they have in Christ and the Holy

Spirit, and Christians who have that power under control.

3. *Self-Control*—The third basic philosophy of life is self-control or temperance. This means the control of *all* personal excess whether it be drunkenness, sexual sin, or even gluttony. Neither does this mean that we are the ones controlling, but it is the Holy Spirit who is being allowed to control. When we go "out-of-control" it is because "self" got in the way.

Once again, here is something the world knows nothing about. Man does not care about self-control. The world's philosophy is "do what feels good, do whatever you want." However, self-control is something every Christian *must* possess.

* * * * *

There we have the "Christian graces" in their *personal, social,* and *philosophical* divisions. How vital each one is! We must allow the Holy Spirit to control every aspect of our lives. We must be allowing Him to produce these Christ-like characteristics in us. In the words of C. I. Scofield in the Scofield Reference Bible: "Christian character is not mere moral nor legal correctness, but the possession and manifestation of the graces of Galatians 5:22-23."

Dear Christian, are you manifesting these "graces"? Are you growing in grace, that is, becoming more like Christ? Are you allowing the Holy Spirit to produce these *graces* in you, not striving and sweating to produce them yourself, but allowing Him full control?

II. GROW IN KNOWLEDGE

May we look now at what it means to grow in knowledge and how we can go about growing in knowledge.

A. The Meaning of "Grow in Knowledge"

We have seen that to "grow in grace" is *to become more like Christ* and as we allow the Holy Spirit to manifest the Christian graces in us we will be more like Christ. Now, to "grow in knowledge" is *to gain a deeper understanding of Christ.* Do you see how they tie together? To be more *like* Him and to know more *of* Him.

May I challenge you to have a desire to grow in knowledge. I dare say that if a person in a particular vocation had the same knowledge of his job after ten years experience that he had on his first day, then he would not be a very good employee. Realistically he would never have lasted the ten years. However, in like manner many Christians today have no more knowledge of Christ and have very little more personal Christian growth now than when they received Christ as Saviour. They know very little more about Him: why He came, what He did, what He accomplished, or what He's still trying to do.

We have already noted Philippians 3:10 earlier in the chapter. Is it our greatest desire to know Him *personally, progressively,* and *powerfully*? To KNOW Him, to gain a deeper understanding of Him, to grow in a personal knowledge of Him should be our greatest desire, not knowing more *about* Him but knowing more *of* Him. This one thing should be our greatest and only desire in life.

The Greek word which is used in Philippians 3:10 and in 2 Peter 3:18 for knowledge is a Greek word which is very important in the Greek language. The word is *ginosko* which means "to know by experience." Another type of knowledge (*oida*) refers to a knowledge gained by someone teaching it to you. However, a *ginosko* type of knowledge indicates a special type of knowledge only obtained by a personal dealing with Jesus Christ. It is a knowledge of a high order and high character, and is a knowledge which always speaks of the Christian's enlightenment. Furthermore, it is a knowledge which is constantly progressing and continuing. As we saw at the beginning of the chapter the verb here is in the present imperative. The *command* of God is to be "continually growing in knowledge."

Oh, how important it is to be growing in our experiential knowledge of Christ! It is vital to realize that we are not striving just to know more *about* Christ, like any other historical figure, but that we are striving to know more *of* Him by experiencing His presence and by getting closer and closer to Him! *That* is a personal experience, and we can never know how joyful, how real, how vital, how successful, and how victorious the Christian life is until we learn to grow in Him.

B. How to "Grow in Knowledge"

The way that God's people are going to grow is through a constant involvement with the Word of God. This is first and foremost accomplished by the preaching of God's Word in the local church. This is something that is tragically being deemphasized in many churches today. However, God has ordained that preaching is the main tool for spreading the Gospel and equipping the saints. Without good expository preaching, Christians, and, therefore, churches, will never deepen nor grow in the Lord.

There is one other way in which we can grow in our knowledge of Christ — READ. How often do Christians these days read a newspaper from front page to back page? How often do we read news magazines, Reader's Digest, numerous periodicals, secular novels, and even material which pertains to our vocation? These are not in themselves wrong, but they may be taking us away from reading God's Word and other Christian books, which are going to feed us, and, therefore, have become sin.

This is the very principle in Hebrews 12:1 that we "lay aside every weight and sin which doth so easily beset us and run with patience the race that is set before us." A "weight" is something which we allow to have so much prominence in our lives that it is slowing down our progress. A weight can keep us away from God's Word, it can keep us away from attendance in God's house, or it can keep us away from actively serving our Saviour.

One of my greatest burdens is that many Christians are allowing God's Word to be crowded out of their lives. The reading of God's Word and other Christian literature no longer has first place in many Christians' lives, that is, if it has any place at all. And by this I do not mean shallow reading about someone's personal experience or some Christian novel. Much of what is being written today may entertain, but it won't produce any real growth. Therefore, read books which will deepen your Christian walk, increase your knowledge, and yield more love for the Lord.

The most horrifying illustration of this that I have ever witnessed was when I was speaking to the owner of a fairly large Christian bookstore which I frequent in Lafayette, Indiana (a city of about 50,000). He said to me, "Did you know that most Christians don't buy books?" I told him I was painfully aware of that. He then said, "Well, here is something you probably don't know. If it wasn't for the Jehovah's Witnesses in this city I couldn't stay in business." I was truly amazed and appalled. Those who deny the very deity of Christ and who are lost in their sin and blindness buy more Christian books than Christians do.

Dear Christian, we shall speak of this subject again in a later chapter, but may I encourage you with all of my heart to *read*. When you stop reading, meditating, and saturating yourself with the Scriptures, you then have broken communication with God, for it is through the Scriptures that He speaks to us as it is through prayer that we speak to Him. When you are not in His Word you will have no real joy, peace, or victory. There may be times when you say, "I just don't have time," but may I again encourage you to make time. There is *nothing* more important than the time we spend with the Lord in His Word and communion in prayer. If you are too busy for these, you are *too busy*. Make time!

In the second appendix of this book is a reprint of a tract I use in the traveling ministry which lists some of the most important reading material for the Christian's growth. I'm so thankful you are reading these words. There are many more God wants you to read and apply. This is the only way we are going to "grow in knowledge."

* * * * *

May we close this chapter with these words by that great expositor G. Campbell Morgan: "Standing in grace and knowledge the soul is in the soil and atmosphere for development. Let there be growth in response to these things." When we are standing in grace and knowledge, we will be in that growing process. Let us truly be "growing in the grace and knowledge of our Lord and Saviour Jesus Christ."

CHAPTER SEVEN

What Is "Faithfulness"?

In 1 Corinthians 4:2, we read:

Moreover, it is required in stewards, that a man be found faithful.

We have thus far said much about Christian service and have at times mentioned faithfulness. However, what exactly *is* faithfulness? Faithfulness is a very important part of this whole area of dedication, for *dedication is where the Christian life BEGINS, but it is by faithfulness that the Christian life is LIVED.*

Our text speaks of a "steward." The context refers directly to the "full-time" minister of the Gospel, but the application certainly implies *every* believer. A steward was an individual who was put in trust of a household. We are told in Genesis 43:19 that Joseph had a steward in his home. Luke 16:1 tells us of the "unjust steward." In like manner, verses such as our text and 1 Peter 4:10 speak of every believer as a steward.

However, what exactly *is* a steward? As we said, a steward was one who was put in charge of a household. He was to keep everything running smoothly. The truth we need to realize immediately about the steward is that nothing belonged to *him*. He took care of all the things that belonged to the master of the house.

Quite often we make the mistake in our finances that the only part which belongs to God is 10 percent. However, the truth is that we are only *stewards* and every penny we have belongs to God. God demands that we give directly to God's work ("as God has prospered us," 1 Cor. 17:2), but *all* of it is His and He has entrusted us to use it wisely, according to His will and guidelines.

Often parents think their children belong to them, but again this is wrong. Children belong to God, "children are an heritage from the Lord; and the fruit of the womb is His reward" (Ps. 127:3). Those children that God has given to us have been entrusted to us to bring them up in the "nurture and admonition of the Lord," to raise them to the glory and honor of God.

We must understand that real faithfulness comes down to the principle that we are stewards to whom *nothing* belongs. Everything belongs to God and He has entrusted all of it to be used for Him. If we will think of ourselves in this, it will do a lot for our Christian lives.

With this in mind, let us now define "faithful." As our text says "it is required in stewards that a man be found faithful." When a man wanted to hire someone to come in and take care of his household, he didn't necessarily ask him if he was good with money, or bookwork, or other financial and social affairs. What he wanted to know was if this man was faithful! He wanted to know if this man was trustworthy and reliable.

The Greek word used here is *pistos* which means "trusted; certain; indubitable." Often people think that faithfulness is the same thing as responsibility, but this is not the case. True faithfulness goes beyond just responsibility and reliability. *The word carries not only the idea of having responsibility, but it assumes that the responsibility will be met without doubt.* For example, the master of a household might say, "Well, I think you are reliable and responsible," but if he believes this man is faithful he would add, "and there's no doubt in my mind that you will meet those responsibilities."

Do you see the difference? True faithfulness assumes that the responsibility that is given to the steward will be carried out without any shadow of a doubt. So, the question we *must* ask ourselves from God's Word is, "Are we faithful?" We may be responsible, but are we faithful? We may be reliable, but are we truly faithful? Can God look at us and say we are faithful "stewards." Does God have any doubt that we will do what He has made us responsible to do?

This type of faithfulness carries with it the idea that we are consistent, constant, continuous, and every day the same. Many Christians are "up and down." One day they're serving the Lord and the next day they are not. This is because they don't have a real grasp on the meaning of faithfulness. *True faithfulness is going to be an outworking of true dedication.*

Let us make a comparison between God's faithfulness and man's faithfulness. Throughout God's Word we see God's faithfulness to us. God has never failed His people. However, we also see that man has been and is equally *un*faithful. To illustrate these truths, let us examine Exodus 12 to 17 and briefly trace the history there. In this section of Scripture we notice how God was faithful to His people, but how they were *un*faithful to Him. We can see in these chapters four basic areas and a three-way comparison between: 1. God's faithfulness to His people; 2. Israel's unfaithfulness to God; and, 3. Our own unfaithfulness as Christians. I would encourage you, the reader, to read Exodus 12 to 17 before we continue.

I. REDEMPTION (Exod. 12:1 to 13:20)

A. God's Faithfulness

First of all we see that God redeemed His people. Now briefly let us note how God redeemed His people.

1. God first redeemed His people *by blood.* Chapter 12, verses 12 and 13 read:

> For I will pass through to the land of Egypt this night, and will smite all the first born in the land of Egypt, both man and beast; and against all the gods of Egypt I will execute judgment: I am the Lord. And the blood shall be to you for a token upon the houses where you are; and when I see the blood, I will pass over you, and the plague shall not be upon you to destroy you, when I smite the land of Egypt.

We, of course, know that this was "The Passover." We know that Christ came as that "Passover Lamb" who came to fulfill that Old Testament picture. What a marvelous fulfillment it was! May we never lose sight of the redemption we have in Christ. May we never grow weary of hearing it. We have been *redeemed,* bought with a price, purchased out of the slave market of sin with the most precious currency the world can ever know—the blood of Jesus Christ.

However, can we imagine the hideous terror in Egypt that night? Only the children of Israel could see and understand what was to happen. What a marvelous redemption it *was* and what a marvelous redemption it *is.*

2. God also redeemed His people *by power.* Chapter 12, verse 37 reads:

> And the children of Israel journeyed from Rameses to Succoth about six hundred thousand on foot that were men, beside children.

As we read down through this passage we see the history of the Exodus. Not only were God's people redeemed by blood, but they were also redeemed by *power.* Only the power of God could have brought an estimated two million Jews out of the land of Egypt.

3. God then redeemed His people *by experience.* Notice Chapter 15, verse 22, through Chapter 16, verse 13. God also miraculously redeemed His people by experience, in that they "experienced" God's provision of water and food.

Think of it! God was truly faithful to His people as He "redeemed" them by blood, by power, and by experience. Redeem means "to purchase by paying a price." God purchased His people.

B. Israel's Unfaithfulness

Please note with me the unfaithfulness of the very people God redeemed. Note Exodus, Chapter 14, verses 11 and 12:

> And they said unto Moses, because there were no graves in Egypt, hast thou taken us away to die in the wilderness? Wherefore hast thou dealt thus with us, to carry us forth out of Egypt? Is not this the word that we did tell thee in Egypt, saying, "Let us alone, that we may serve the Egyptians?" For it had been better for us to serve the Egyptians, than that we should die in the wilderness.

Beloved Christian, can you imagine this? Here is the nation of Israel that God has brought out of the bondage and slavery of Egypt now saying that they wished He would have left them alone!

May we note that they were *unthankful for redemption.* Please remember that they were unthankful for that which God had done for them.

C. What About Us?

We look at the Israelites and say, "Those Hebrews! How in the world could they be so unthankful?" But how often are we just as unthankful and just as unfaithful as they were? We also have been redeemed. We have been "bought with a price" (1 Cor. 6:20 and 7:23) and have quite literally been "redeemed out of the slave market of sin." We have been redeemed by *blood* (the blood of Jesus Christ on calvary); we have been redeemed by *power* (the power of His resurrection); and we have been redeemed by *experience* (that is, we experience the victory over sin and the provision of God in our daily lives).

Nonetheless, how often are we unthankful for it all? We show an unthankfulness when we live like we are back in bondage and allow sin to reign in our lives. We show unthankfulness when we allow other things to take first place over the things of Christ. At the end of this chapter we want to examine some important principles which will help us remember some basic areas of faithfulness. Are we *unthankful for our redemption?*

II. GUIDANCE (Exod. 13:21-22)

A. God's Faithfulness

We also see that God was faithful to His people in His guidance of them. Note Chapter 12, verses 21 and 22:

> And the Lord went before them by day in a pillar of a cloud, to lead them the way; and by night in a pillar of fire, to give them light; to go by day and night. He took not away the pillar of the cloud by day, nor the pillar of fire by night, from among the people.

God was faithful in His guidance. Not one time did He leave His children alone in the wilderness! Think of it! Here is true guidance. He "went before" His people.

Without "spiritualizing," may we look at that cloud and that fire as types of foreviews of the Holy Spirit and His guidance in the believer's life. Not once did He take His guidance away, and likewise God will not allow us to be without His presence. Oh, we may run away from Him, we may ignore His presence, we may turn away from Him, but never will He "leave us nor forsake us" (Heb. 13:5). He always "goes before" us. He is not behind us pushing us, nor is He ahead of us dragging us. He goes before to lead us.

One of the great verses about the Holy Spirit is found in John 16:13 where we are told that "He will guide us in all truth." This "Comforter will abide with us forever" and He is there to *guide* us in all things. Oh, how faithful God is!

B. Israel's Unfaithfulness

We have already noted Exodus 14:11 and 12 and how Israel was *unthankful for redemption.* However, in the same context we see that they were also *unyielded in guidance.* Continue to remember these points.

Oh, but some would say, "Now wait a minute. The people *did* follow. They went out of Egypt and followed Moses right into the desert." Yes, but they complained every step of the way. They *went,* but they were not *yielded.*

C. What About Us?

Yes, the children of Israel went, just like many Christians today go and do what the pastor asks, just like many Christians come to church. Quite often, though, our service is motivated not out of *yieldedness to God,* but out of pressure from someone else's authority.

This brings us right back to the very thrust of our study—the total surrender and dedication of the believer to Christ. This is what the children of Israel needed. Yes, they were in the Old Testament economy, but the parallel is the same. They needed to yield to divine control. They complained at every turn and spoke evil of the leadership. Likewise, many dear Christians today complain and criticize God's man and show that they have never dedicated themselves to God. God has had to judge Israel down through the ages and this is why they are scattered now into all the world—because they would not yield. Therefore, we as Christians in *this* age can see the danger of an unyielded life. Are we *unyielding in guidance*?

III. DELIVERANCE (Exod. 14:1-15:21)

A. God's Faithfulness

God was also faithful to His people in that He delivered them. Chapter 14, verses 21 and 22 read:

> And Moses stretched out his hand over the sea; and the Lord caused the sea to go back by a strong east wind all that night, and made the sea dry land, and the waters were divided. And the children of Israel went into the midst of the sea upon the dry ground; and the waters were a wall unto them on their right hand and on their left.

Can you imagine the scene? Many years ago the special effects of Hollywood produced this scene in the movie "The Ten Commandments," and how amazing they made it look. However, can we imagine how it *really* looked?

Of course, the liberals say they actually only crossed in knee-deep water. However, as someone said long ago, "We can still praise the Lord, for this means He drowned all the army of Pharoah in knee-deep water!" So much for the liberals, but what we need to see is that God delivered His people. He delivered them from the bondage they were *in* and the danger they *confronted.* God was faithful!

B. Israel's Unfaithfulness

Now, when we again examine Chapter 14, verses 21 and 22, we not only want to remember that Israel was *unthankful for redemption* and *unyielded in guidance,* but that they were also *ungodly in deliverance.* By this we need to understand what God has done. He has brought them out of the land of Egypt and He has delivered them by His power, but they still live in ungodliness. As we see in their later history, they built a golden calf (Exod. 32) and bowed down and worshiped it instead. In so doing, they were only concerned with ungodly pleasure and wickedness for they "sat down to eat and to drink, and rose up to play" (Exod. 32:6).

C. What About Us?

In like manner, as we have already been challenged in previous chapters, are we living ungodly? Down through the sixth chapter of Romans, God says we are dead to sin and all those who are dead to sin are *freed* from sin. There is no supposed "old nature" that has a strangulation hold on us so that we can't help but sin. As we have noted, this defeats the Christian life. We sin because we *choose* to sin. We will look at this in more detail in the next chapter.

The children of Israel were ungodly in their deliverance. God brought them *out* of bondage but they wanted to go *back* to bondage. Likewise, often we as Christians do the same. God brought us out of bondage, but we go right back into it. This is the point of Hebrews 12:1:

> Wherefore, seeing we also are compassed about with so great a cloud of witnesses, let us lay aside every weight, and the sin which doth so easily beset us, and let us run with patience the race that is set before us.

The "weights" spoken of are encumbrances; things which in themselves are not sin, but things that become sin because they keep us from growth and maturity.

As Lazarus came forth from the grave by the command of the Lord Jesus (John 11:43-44), Jesus said to those around Him, "Loose him and let him go." They took off of him the graveclothes, the things which showed that he was dead, and put them aside to show that now he was alive. There was no reason to keep on the evidences of death, for he was alive! Are we *ungodly in deliverance*?

IV. PROVISION (Exod. 15:22-17:7)

A. God's Faithfulness

Last we see that God was faithful in His provision. Note Chapter 16, verses 14 and 15:

> And when the dew that lay was gone up, behold, upon the face of the wilderness there lay a small round thing, as small as the hoar frost on the ground. And when the children of Israel saw it, they said to one another, It is manna; for they knew not what it was. And Moses said unto them, This is the bread which the Lord hath given us to eat.

We have here the English word "manna" which doesn't really tell us anything until we know the source of the word. It comes from two Hebrew words, *man hu.* "Manna" is not a translation at all. The translators merely took the Hebrew letters and gave them English equivalents, making *man hu* into "manna."

The Hebrew words literally mean, "What is it?" The children of Israel came out, looked all around, and saw this small round thing laying with the dew. With puzzled faces they said, "What is it?" Moses' answer was simple, "It's what God has provided." We have come to call it "manna" in the English, but may we actually call it what it was—then again we don't know what it was. *All they needed to know and all we need to know is it was God's provision.*

B. Israel's Unfaithfulness

What was the attitude of the children of Israel? May we simply read Chapter 15, verse 24, and Chapter 16, verses 2 and 3:

> And the people murmured against Moses, saying, What shall we drink? And the whole congregation . . . murmured against Moses and Aaron in the wilderness. And . . . said unto them, Would that we had died by the hand of the Lord in the land of Egypt, when we sat by the flesh pots, and when we did eat bread to the full; for ye have brought us forth into this wilderness, to kill this whole assembly with hunger.

Both of these instances happened *before* the fact of God's provision. Therefore, in addition to being *unthankful for redemption, unyielded in guidance,* and *ungodly in deliverance,* the children of Israel were now *unbelieving for provision.* They did not believe God.

C. What About Us?

How often are we as believers unbelieving in God's provision? How often do we doubt that God *will* or even *can* provide our needs? We have already examined the promise in Philippians 4:19, "And my God shall supply all your needs according to His riches in glory by Christ Jesus." How often do we worry about temporal matters and, therefore, manifest unbelief?

* * * * *

Dear Christian, are you really faithful? Are you:

Thankful or unthankful for redemption?
Yielded or unyielded for guidance?
Godly or ungodly in deliverance?
Believing or unbelieving for provision?

I would like to close this chapter with a brief study of some areas in which God desires our faithfulness. The easiest way to do this is with a simple acrostic of the word: F A I T H - F U L.

1. *Fruitfulness.* Are we really faithful in living a fruitful Christian life? It is tragic that, these days, many say that the only "fruit" of the Christian life is seeing people come to Christ, and if a Christian is not seeing people get saved, then he is not fruitful. However, this attitude is wrong, for it is not our responsibility to see people *come* to Christ, but, rather, it is our responsibility to be a faithful *witness* of Christ. Results are not up to us, for it is "God who gives the increase" (1 Cor. 3:7). The word "witness" in Acts 1:8 is the plural form of *martus* which means "one who testifies" and shows one who doesn't just talk about Christ, but it is one who manifests Christ to those around them by the way he lives. A witness doesn't just say it with the *lips,* but he also shows it with the *life.*

It is also tragic that many today emphasize the term "soul-winning," for again this puts the stress on the *results* instead of the witness. There are even "soul-winning clubs" which have Christians competing with one another for winning people to Christ and have all sorts of prizes for these so-called "soul win-ners." The term comes from Proverbs 11:30, ". . . he that win-neth souls is wise." However, the Hebrew word does not neces-sarily imply "to win" but rather "to contend for" showing that a truly wise man will be contending (working) for souls. It literally states that "he that is wise contends for souls," not that "he that contends is wise." Wisdom must come first or we will not witness properly.

It is quite interesting to notice that men are continually com-ing up with "new methods for winning people to Christ." There is this program and that program, and it seems that men think they can improve on God's revealed method. God told us that we have been sent forth to be witnesses of Christ in our everyday life. If God's men, that is, preachers and teachers, would just teach this truth, then we would see people come to Christ as God gives the increase.

Oh, how important evangelism is! Some years ago I heard Vance Havner say, "Evangelism is to Christianity what veins are to our body. If you cut it, it must bleed evangelism." However, may our evangelism be done God's way. That "crown of rejoicing" which will be given at the Judgment Seat of Christ (1 Thess. 2:19) will be given to those who have been faithful witnesses of Christ, not to those who have had great results.

When speaking of fruitfulness, there are at least three areas which come to mind. One area is *converts*. In Romans 1:13 Paul encourages, "Now I would not have you ignorant, brethren, that oftentimes I proposed to come unto you . . . that I might have some fruit among you also, even as among the Gentiles." There were still those in Rome who needed Christ and Paul wanted to see them saved. Another area of fruitfulness is *character*, that is, seeing a deepening of Christian character and growth in ourselves and other Christians as we show forth those "Christian graces" in Galatians 5:22-23. One other area of faithfulness is *conduct*, that is, that we may have "fruit unto holiness" (Rom. 6:22; Phil. 1:11). We are being fruitful when we live holy.

2. *Attitudes.* Are we being faithful in having the right attitudes? Again those "Christian graces" in Galatians 5:22-23 come to mind. These are the greatest attitudes a Christian should have. *Attitudes produce actions* and if we have these attitudes we are going to be blessed of God.

3. *Instruction.* Are we being faithful to the instruction of God's Word? Which of the following is true of your life? a) "I am thankful for the opportunity to hear the Word of God preached and taught"; b) "My greatest desire is to hear the Word of God preached and taught"; c) "I have a hunger and thirst for the Word of God that goes beyond just hearing it preached and taught." While the first two are very commendable, the third one is what God requires. We have already touched on this subject and will do so indepth in a later chapter, but our instruction in God's Word is vital and God demands our faithfulness.

4. *Thanksgiving.* Are we faithful in thanking God for what He has given us? We teach children to say "thank you," but quite often we don't thank God for His blessings on our lives. If we would discipline ourselves to sit down with a pen and paper and prayerfully write down all that God has given us, I dare say we would be busy for many hours. I am sure a new vision of a gracious, loving God would be ours at the end of those hours. Oh, may we thank Him! Thanksgiving is often coupled with praise and worship throughout the Scripture. May we "walk in Christ; rooted and built up in Him and established in the faith. As ye have taught, *abounding with thanksgiving*" (Col. 2:6-7, emphasis mine).

5. *House of God.* Are we faithful to "God's house"? We do not mean a physical structure. A church is not a "building" but rather "an assembly" made up of believers. However, when making this distinction there are some these days who belittle the church building which in a sense *is* "God's house" since God's people are in it. Some say the building has no importance. I've heard some say that it is not a "sanctuary" we meet in but an "auditorium." Therefore, it seems to me, it has no better place than a movie theater, for that, too, is an auditorium.

No, the church building is not "the dwelling place of God," for He indwells the believer. However, there *is* something special about the place where believers meet to worship, learn, and fellowship. It is not a place for children to run or adults to socialize. It's not the same as every other building. It's a place for reverence, not that it is the thing *to be* worshiped, but rather it is the place *for* worship.

While the building *is* important there is also the danger of giving it first place. Some think it has to be a big cathedral with carpet, chandeliers, padded pews, stained glass, and all the other trimmings. However, it is not the type of structure that matters, for the early churches met in homes. What matters is the spiritual atmosphere in the church.

Nonetheless, the question remains, "Are we faithful to God's house"? Is our church attendance important to us? Do we feel a void when we are unable to attend? How distressing it is that many Christians do not consider their church attendance important. There are many things which can come before a midweek service, a Sunday evening service, or even a Sunday morning service. As we have already noticed in studying worldliness, many Christians allow the world to dictate about working on Sunday. They say, "Oh, I *have* to work," but may I lovingly submit, *no, they don't!*

While we do not live under the law and no longer adhere to the Sabbath, we have still missed the spirit of the law. There are many who try so hard to make sure we are theologically correct, and don't want to get shackled by the *letter* of the law in this dispensation of grace, that they miss the *spirit* of the law. These people have missed the attitude in which Exodus 20:8 was spoken:

> Remember the Sabbath day and keep it holy.

Yes, by the *letter* of the law this is the seventh day of the week (Saturday) and is to be set aside for rest. However, the *spirit* of the law, that is, the attitude behind it, is that the whole week is spent in other activities, but one day a week should be set aside for rest and worship. Because of the resurrection of Christ on the first day of the week (Sunday), then our day of rest and worship should be on Sunday.

There is a command given to *all* believers in Hebrews 10:25 which many Christians totally ignore:

> Not forsaking the assembling of yourselves together, as the manner of some is, but exhorting one another, and so much the more, as ye see the day approaching.

What a marvelous verse! The writer, who many believe to be Paul, is telling us that we *must* not shirk our responsibility to attend God's house, for at the time he was writing many were doing just that. We should "exhort," that is, to be encouraging each other to be faithful as we see the coming of Christ draw nearer. Some of the blame for the lack of church attendance is fault of the pulpit ministry and the lack of sound, practical biblical exposition as we will see again in a later chapter.

Oh, may we see how important it is that "God's people need to be in God's house on God's day to hear God's Word." We can think of many excuses but that is all they are—excuses. A simple rule we can use for our attendance is: *Never miss unless absolutely necessary.* And every Christian does know the difference between an *excuse* and a *reason.*

6. *Finances.* Are we being faithful in our finances. The New Testament principle goes far beyond the tithe, for in 1 Corinthians 16:2 we read:

> Upon the first day of the week let every one of you lay by him in store, as God hath prospered him, that there be no gatherings when I come.

God wants our financial support to go to the local church. Everything we have belongs to God, not just 10 percent of it. However, still more important is the fact that most Christians *can* give more than 10 percent because of how God has prospered them (1 Cor. 16:2). In all sincerity we should get as far away as we can from this attitude of "tithe." We should give abundantly to our Lord for He has given abundantly to us.

So, are we being faithful in our finances? Are we giving as much as we should or could? There are at least three major areas which must be taken care of financially. In order of importance God wants local churches to take care of:

a. The pastor. A church is first and foremost responsible for the pastor. There are those today who think a pastor should work outside the church to either support himself fully or partially. Others think that this practice is not ideal but still necessary. However, God tells us in 1 Corinthians 9:17-18 that those who preach the Gospel should live by means of the Gospel. Notice verse 14:

> Even so hath the Lord ordained that they who preach the Gospel should live of the Gospel.

This is what the entire context is teaching. Paul also encourages young Pastor Timothy that "the labourer is worthy of his reward" (1 Tim. 5:18, 2 Tim. 2:6). A pastor who is doing his job as God intended needs full-time support from his church. Yes, there will be special circumstances, but the first goal of a church is not a building, a youth program, or any other program, but rather a full-time pastor. He that labors in the work "must be first partaker of the fruits" (2 Tim. 2:6).

b. Missions. A church is then responsible to give to missions, to support those missionaries, home and foreign, who are doing God's work. Churches should have a mission budget and Christians should be concerned about those on the different fields. God's people should not give their money to the world's organizations, such as "The United Fund," among others. For one thing, people have no idea where that money goes. However, more importantly these organizations only deal with the physical, which will never change the heart. Giving to Christian missions, *those who start local churches* home and abroad and preach the Word, is God's intention. We must give to that which will change lives from *within*.

c. The church building. The last financial responsibility is the building in which we meet. It must meet the *need* but must never be allowed to cause *neglect* to other priorities. It may be *favorable* but never *first* in our affection, for, as I have seen before, God may destroy it by *fire*. And above all, God's house must be *godly,* not *gaudy.*

7. *Uprightness.* Are we being faithful in holiness? We will deal with this in more detail in a later chapter, but do we believe *in* and live *by* God's standards of morality? What a blessed verse is Psalm 143:10:

> Teach me to do Thy will . . . lead me into the land of uprightness.

David knew quite well the consequences of sin by what he went through because of his sin with Bathsheba. He knew that holiness was literally "a place to dwell" and *we* dwell in Christ's righteousness, truly "the land of uprightness."

8. *Labor.* Are we being faithful in our labor for the Lord? How much *time* do we devote to Him in direct service? Are there *talents* or other abilities which God wants us to be using for His glory and praise? We can thank Him that He will not "forget our work and labour of love which we show toward His name" (1 Cor. 3:8).

Some of these areas will be emphasized in other studies. However, what we want to grasp is the need for *real* faithfulness, for, beloved Christian, remember, *the only thing God will bless is faithfulness.* He will not bless a method, an idea, a ministry, or anything else except consistent faithfulness. Throughout the Scriptures we see that God blessed men because they were FAITHFUL. *The Christian life BEGINS with dedication, but it is lived through FAITHFULNESS.* Are *you* faithful?

Beloved Saviour, You have been, are,
and will always be the same;
May I likewise be faithful
To Your work and Your Name.

CHAPTER EIGHT

The Encouragements of John

In the first epistle of John we find four most encouraging verses:

These things write we unto you that your joy may be full (1:4).

My little children, these things write I unto you, that ye sin not. And if any man sin, we have an advocate with the Father, Jesus Christ the righteous (2:1).

These things have I written unto you that believe on the name of the Son of God, that ye may know that ye have eternal life, and that ye may believe on the name of the Son of God (5:13).

These things have I written unto you concerning them that seduce you (2:26).

The main theme of John's epistle is "fellowship in God's family." It is a "family letter" written from the Father to His "little children" who are in the world. When we meditate on the language John uses we quickly see that this letter, with the possible exception of the Song of Solomon, is the most intimate writing in all the Scriptures.

With this theme in mind, John states *four* reasons why he wrote this letter. Four times he uses the phrase "these things have I written unto you" or similar phrases. It is upon these four occurrences that we see John's major encouragements to the believer who is God's "little child." There are a few other times when this phrase is used but there are only four basic thoughts that John emphasizes.

I. Encouragement to Joy

The first encouragement John gives the New Testament believer is one of joy. "These things have been written unto you that your joy may be full." We have examined this principle of joy already. We say that it is something which is absolute and independent of circumstances, while happiness is relative and totally circumstantial.

To understand why John wrote this statement in verse 4, we must look at the three verses which precede it. He speaks there of Jesus Christ:

That which was from the beginning, which we have heard, which we have seen with our eyes, which we have looked upon, and our hands have handled of the Word of life (For the life was manifested, and we have seen it, and bear witness, and show unto you that eternal life, which was with the Father, and was manifested unto us). That which we have seen and heard declare we unto you, that ye also may have fellowship with us; and truly our fellowship is with the Father, and with His Son, Jesus Christ.

Then, we come to verse 4: "*These* things were written that your joy may be full."

What then is our joy? Our joy is our fellowship with Jesus and our fellowship then with the Father. John is telling us that joy comes by fellowship; fellowship with the Father and the Son, and, as verse 3 also indicates, fellowship with other believers. It is our *fellowship* in the family that is the cause of real joy.

However, what is "fellowship"? Some witty individual has said, "Fellowship is two fellows in the same ship." It is fascinating to note that often the more clever we try to be with God's Word the sillier we show ourselves to be. God doesn't need our cleverness or "triteness." What He needs is for us to take the Word as it is given. The Greek word for fellowship here means, "joint participation in a common interest and activity." You may have "two fellows in the same ship" but their interests and activities may be completely the opposite.

Many Christians these days think they are having fellowship if they have a "church dinner," or some other church-oriented activity, or by having coffee together after the Sunday evening service. Now, these are all well and good, but they are not necessarily "fellowship" in the strict sense of the word. The implication of the Scriptures is always towards "spiritual fellowship," that is, joint participation in common spiritual interests and activities. However, how often are our so-called "fellowship times" spent in discussing politics, sports, "household hints," and other such things? Again, none of these are necessarily wrong. However, are they the only things that occupy our time?

God wants Christians to have true fellowship with Him and other believers. He wants us to have a joint participation in common spiritual interests and activities. The type of interests and activities He desires are a love and desire for His Word, a deep prayer life, sacrificial giving, and personal witness. Think of it! Our fellowship, our interests and activity should be on the things of Christ!

Another marvelous blessing in this verse is that our joy may be *full*. To get the full impact of the word we must look at it in the light of the original language. We have already seen the great importance of the aorist tense, that tense which shows a once-for-all past action. However, "full" is in the perfect tense which is the tense that shows past action with an emphasis on the result. A simple illustration will explain. Let us think of the words "getting married" as in the perfect tense. We only get married once (past action), but the result of that once-for-all action continues on.

In like manner, our joy is *full*. It has been filled in the past by Jesus entering our life and continues in that state of fullness. An expanded translation of the verse by Kenneth Wuest goes this way:

And these things, as for us, we are writing in order that our joy, having been filled completely full in times past, may persist in that state of fullness through the present time.

Oh, what joy we have in Christ! As we saw earlier this is not *emotionalism* but true *enthusiasm.* That joy was given in the past. We have walked with the Saviour, we have talked with Him, and our faith is in Him. He has given us eternal life. *That* is when our joy was given, but now it continues in its fullness.

Oh, may we never leave that joy! This is what the problem was with the believers in the Church at Ephesus in Revelation, Chapter 1. They were doing great things for God. In verses 2 and 3 the Lord gives a seven-fold *commendation* of them. He said He knew their works, He knew their toil, He knew their patience, He knew they did not tolerate ungodliness, He knew they discerned false teachers, He knew they endured persecution, and He knew that they would not allow themselves to become discouraged.

Nonetheless, His *complaint* against them was that even though they were accomplishing much they still had *left their first love.* They did not "lose" their first love as some might think. They did not misplace it as they would misplace a piece of clothing. They actually "left" their first love. The Greek tells us that they deserted or forsook their first love. This first love is the love of espousal, the love of romance. When we leave our first love we have left the joy, the thrill, and the simplicity of our personal relationship with Christ. Many married couples have had this happen in their marriages. In all their busyness they leave behind the joy and thrill of their relationship. Many Christians do the same with Christ. So often in our busyness and in the hustle-and-bustle of life, we forsake the Saviour. We forget what He has done for us.

Our Dear Saviour came,
    the power of sin to destroy;
Oh, the fellowship we now have
    in His wonderful fullness of joy.

Dear Christian, never leave your joy in Christ. Never leave that thrill of your salvation. Never leave that excitement and thankfulness you knew at your conversion.

II. ENCOURAGEMENT TO HOLINESS

The second encouragement John gives to the New Testament believer is one of holiness. At this point we want to deal with a subject which is of the utmost importance to living the Christian life. We will note John's teaching on holiness and see how it parellels the teaching of Paul back in Romans.

We notice first of all that John's tone has changed. His manner of speech is very tender. He uses the more personal pronoun "I" instead of the more formal pronoun "we." His tone is personal and affectionate as he addresses these believers as "little children." Why did he use this term? As we all recall from the Gospels, John was "the apostle whom Jesus loved." There was a reason for that. It seems that John was the type of man who really understood what love was and understood the relationship between a father and his "little children." John, no doubt, captured that term from our Lord in John 12:33 and really knew its meaning. When we think of the Apostle John we should always think of a loving and tender man for he was speaking to believers *then* and is still speaking to believers *now* as "little children."

John assumes this tone because he is about to give them a solemn warning. He wants to take the sting out of what he is about to say and wants to stop any opposition which might arise. His statement is:

My little children, these things write I unto you, that ye sin not. And if any man sin, we have an advocate with the Father, Jesus Christ the righteous.

Before we go any further, let us ask the question, "Why does God hate sin?" Yes, we know that sin held Christ on the cross. We know that God cannot look upon sin, for it is contrary to His nature. We know that God is pure and cannot tolerate impurity. We know that sin is the breaking of God's law, therefore, separating us from Him. We also know other theological truths about sin. However, there is a much more personal reason why God hates sin. A dear pastor friend of mine put it this way, "God hates sin because He loves people, and sin hurts people." How simple! Sin destroys everything it touches, and this is why God hates it.

This is why John says, "Don't sin." As we have already seen, John says this in a tone which will stop any opposition which would be forming in people's minds. There were (and still are) two possible perversions of John's statement, "Don't sin." John knew there were two basic ways which his statement could be perverted.

The first perversion was, "If we in this life can never be done with sin, then why should we strive for holiness?" The second perversion was, "If forgiveness for sin is so easy, then why dread falling into sin?"

There are today these two perversions of John's statement. The parallel today of the first perversion is, "We as believers still have within us an 'old nature' which makes us unable to keep from sinning." The second parallel is that "We as believers are on our way to heaven and so we do can anything we want," that is, we have a "license to sin."

To both of these John says, "No." In essence he says, "I am not writing these things to either discourage you to holy living or to condone sinning, but, on the contrary, in order that you may not sin." What seems at human glance to be a paradox is really a marvelous spiritual truth which gives the believer real victory. Let us examine John's teaching in depth.

Note what John says, "If any man sin." Now, if we look at that statement only in the English we are going to be a little foggy in our understanding. For first John says, "Don't sin," and now he says, "If any man sin." This seems to be a contradiction. We know that we do still sin so why does John say, "Don't sin"? Is John trying to confuse us? Or, is he trying to be theologically clever? Of course, he is not doing either one.

This phrase "If any man sin" is in the aorist subjunctive in the Greek. The aorist is once-for-all action and the subjunctive mood is action which can possibly happen. The best way to express the subjunctive mood is with the word "if." Therefore, the best translation of this phrase is, "if any man commits an act of sin." It speaks of an *act* of sin, not *continuous* sin. John is showing us here that sin in the believer's life is infrequent, not habitual.

Note also Chapter 3, verse 6. This verse literally says, "Whosoever abides in Him does not habitually practice sin." Here we have the present tense showing continuous action. The man who is truly in Christ, truly born again, does not live in sin. The rest of the verse tells us, "whosoever sinneth hath not seen him, neither known him." The man who is continually sinning, who habitually sins over and over, and who has no remorse for his sin shows that *he is not born again.*

Note one more verse in Chapter 3. Again, literally rendered, verse 9 tells us that "whosoever has been born of God does not habitually commit sin for His seed continually remains in him, and he cannot habitually sin, because he has been born of God." Here we see that one who is truly "born of God" (once-for-all act) cannot habitually commit sin. The words "His seed" refer to the divine life the believer possesses. This seed of divine life remains in us continually and makes it impossible for us to continually live in sin. God's seed causes us to hate sin and love righteousness.

These verses do great damage to the viewpoint that Christians have "license to sin." It also does damage to those dear Christians who reject the security of the believer because they think that anyone who believes in "eternal security" believes in a license to sin. They say "Once you people are saved, you're always saved, so you can do what you want to." Not so! John tells us that a man who commits sin habitually and continuously day in and day out with no sorrow or consciousness of sin is lost. That person was never saved! However, a man who has truly been born again no longer lives in sin.

Another question many ask on this subject is, "Well, how about the man who was saved but then 'backslid' for many years. He went back to the old life?" According to the Scriptures, that man was never saved—he made a profession, but he never had the possession. Habitual sin shows a lost condition.

Now let us continue in Chapter 2, verse 1. If we do commit an *act* of sin, not habitual, but one act, we then have "an advocate with the Father, Jesus Christ the righteous." How often do we have a wrong attitude, a wrong motive, a selfish desire, or say a cross word, or do something else which is displeasing to God? These are the realities of every believer and are not habitual, continuous sin; but single acts of sin which happen when the Holy Spirit does not have control of our minds and bodies.

Dear Christian, when you sin and it grieves your heart, or when you read God's Word or hear it preached, and realize there is something in your life which does not belong there, it is because you are "born of God." When there is sin in your life, it grieves your heart and pricks your spirit because the Spirit of God is in you. This does not happen to the "habitual sinner" because he is lost. However, it does happen to the *true* believer.

It is then that you apply 1 John 1:9:

> If we confess our sins; He is faithful and just to forgive us our sins and to cleanse us from all unrighteousness.

The Greek for "confess" is *homologeo, homo* meaning "same" and *log* meaning *"word."* Therefore, to confess means to say the same words about sin that God does. In other words, call sin *SIN.* Don't water it down. Call it what it is. It is only when we truly and sorrowfully confess our sin that God then forgives.

It is at this time, when the believer commits an act of sin, that he has "an advocate with the Father, Jesus Christ the righteous." The word "advocate" is the Greek *parakletos,* where we get the English word paraclete. It means "one who is called alongside to aid." It is Jesus who is our paraclete, our "defense attorney," who comes to our aid when we commit an act of sin. It was Jesus who through His work on Calvary, gave forgiveness of sin. It was Jesus, who by His death, burial and resurrection, gave us victory over the *penalty* and *power* of sin.

Let us parallel John's teaching here with Paul's teaching in Romans, Chapters 6, 7, and 8. These three chapters are of the utmost importance in any teaching on holiness. In Romans, Chapter 6, we are told that God has declared us dead to sin by judicial act because of our identification with Christ's death. The entire sixth chapter speaks of a totally complete judicial act of God which was done in the past. Paul silenced the same perversion that John silenced. In verse 2, Paul says:

> How shall we that are dead to sin live any longer in it?

Verse 3 then tells us that we were "baptized," that is, immersed or placed into His death in a completed act. Then verses 4 and 5 show that as we were buried in His death we were also given life by His resurrection. A parallel verse to these is that marvelous text in Galatians 2:20 which literally reads, "with Christ I have been crucified and I live no more, but Christ lives in me . . . ."

However, the most blessed verse of all in Romans 6, is verse 6. I would like to give the expanded translation of the verse along with the explanation of each phrase that is given in Dr. J.

Sidlow Baxter's book, *A New Call to Holiness,* a classic work on this subject:

Our old man	all that we were by position and relation to Adam, with all our condemnation;
was crucified with Him	was judged and executed in the once-for-all death of Christ;
that the body of sin	the whole Adam humanity was guilty before God;
might be destroyed	completely done away in the judicial reckoning of God;
that we should no longer be in bondage to sin	no longer in *legal* bondage thru *judicial* guilt.

What a marvelous truth! As we examine Romans 6 we find that every verb which speaks of our identification with Christ is in a *past* tense. We are dead to sin, freed from sin, no longer chained to sin. This destroys the second perversion of John's statement "Don't sin." Many teach that we have within us an "old nature" which has some strangulation hold on us so that we cannot help but sin. However, this is not what God reveals in His Word. There is no old nature but the "old man" which was totally destroyed by the death and resurrection of Christ, so that we are free from the bondage and power that sin once had over us. One who is truly born again *cannot* habitually commit sin because he is dead to sin.

Ah, but now some would ask, "Why then do we still sin?" Others would ask "Does all this mean that we are sinlessly perfect right now?" The answer to both of these is in Romans, Chapter 7. Paul shows us in Chapter 6 that we are freed from the legal guilt and judicial bondage of sin, but now in Chapter 7 he explains that there is still within our nature something called "the flesh." The flesh is our own *selfish propensities,* or our own self-will—what we want. This is not an "old nature," for God made us with one nature that He is trying to "continually transform by the renewing of our minds." However, still with the human nature is "the flesh," that drive to sin which is ever present.

How then do we get victory over the flesh? This is the next

logical question, and the answer is in Romans, Chapter 8. Here we are told that the indwelling Holy Spirit gives us victory over our flesh. Note verses 8 and 10:

And those who are in the flesh cannot please God. However, you are not in the flesh but in the Spirit, if indeed the Spirit of God dwells in you . . . (NASV).

Here we have the whole picture. God is telling us that He has given us victory and complete freedom over the penalty and power of sin. However, still within us is the flesh which drives us to sin when we give our permission. However, still further, we have been given the indwelling Holy Spirit to give us victory over the flesh when we allow *Him* to control.

Beloved Christian, how dare we ever say that we can't help but sin! We don't have to sin! I have heard it put this way, *We do not have the inability to sin, but we do have the ability not to sin.* Did you get it? Read it again. God has given us real victory. Let's claim it.

I have only been able to briefly deal with this topic of holiness. I would again recommend the classic works by J. Sidlow Baxter. His three-book trilogy is of the upmost importance for every believer: *A New Call to Holiness, His Deeper Work in Us,* and *Our High Calling.*

III. ENCOURAGEMENT TO ASSURANCE

John's third encouragement to us is one of assurance of salvation. This is most thrilling, for "these things have been written that we may know that we have eternal life" (v. 13).

To understand this verse we must understand the relationship between John's *Gospel* and the first *Epistle* of John. There are recorded in the Gospel of John seven miracles which are signs of Christ's incarnation and prove He is the Son of God, God in the flesh. John tells us the purpose of the book in Chapter 10, verses 30 and 31:

And many other signs [in addition to the ones already given] truly did Jesus in the presence of His disciples, which are not written in this book; but these are written, that ye might believe that Jesus is the Christ, the Son of God; and that believing ye might have eternal life.

So, the purpose of John's Gospel was so we might believe in

Christ's incarnation and have eternal life.

Now, why was this epistle written? The answer is in our text. It was written not merely that we have eternal life by believing, but it was written that we may *know* we have eternal life. This first epistle supplements the Gospel. It is the personal application of the Gospel. God not only wants us to *have* eternal life, but He also wants us to *know* we have it.

Contrary to the belief of many, we *can* know beyond any doubt that we are on our way to heaven. In my first pastorate some years ago, I would speak to people in the community and ask them—"Are you sure you are on your way to heaven?" Often the response was, "Well, I hope so." I would then explain to them verse 13 of Chapter 5 of First John, and then ask them the question again and would get the same answer. In those early days of ministry I sometimes got discouraged because people refused to see that they *could* really know they were saved.

Still others today reject the doctrine of the security of the believer and call it by that most unfortunate term "once saved, always saved." In the first appendix of this book is a discussion of a number of scriptural proofs of the security of the believer. How tragic it is that many believers live a whole life with no assurance, believing that they could be saved one moment and lost the next. How can we fall from grace? How can we fall from "unmerited favour"? How can we become unjustified? How can *eternal* life not be eternal? If we can lose our salvation, Christianity is no better than all the religions of the world, for they are all based on works. The same power of God that saved us is the same power that keeps us.

Nonetheless, many ask, "What about the one who is involved in sin, but says he is a Christian?" We dealt with that earlier. There is a great difference between the single act and habitual sin.

Look at our text one last time. "These things have I written unto you ... that ye may know ...." Here we have action which is *possible*. It is possible that you may keep on knowing (present tense). The action here is possible, not definite, for it is based upon our decision. We *can* continually know, if we want to know. Note also that we may know *we have*, present tense again. Putting it together, "We can know we have salvation day in, day out, progressively, every single day of our lives, and continually every day of our lives."

The type of knowledge spoken of here ("that you may know") is an *oida* knowledge which, as we saw in an earlier chapter, refers to knowledge gained; not by experience, but by someone teaching it to you or through other study. These things have been *written*. We can read them and see God prove to us that we have eternal life.

Again, for a deeper discussion of these thoughts, go to the first appendix.

IV. ENCOURAGEMENT TO BEWARE

John's final encouragement to us is to "beware of those who would seduce us" (2:26). I urge you to read the context of the chapter, verses 18-24. We must at this point understand a philosophy which was present in John's day. It was called "gnosticism." Though the heresy is not named by John, he nonetheless reveals it by what he says, and even though it didn't reach full-bloom until the Second Century, it still existed in its early form two to three decades before John's death.

Gnosticism supposedly had some "special revelation" superior to normal Christianity, handed down mystically from Christ but known only to some "inner circle." During John's day it had begun to make its way into the churches. Basically it was a philosophy of existence or being. It stemmed largely from the old Greek dualism which taught there is a "good god" and a "bad god" always in conflict. In gnosticism, God was good and matter was evil and the intellect was supreme while faith and conduct were of little importance.

Technically, gnosticism does not exist today, but men's philosophies never really change. We can note some striking parallels between gnosticism and the philosophies of today.

1. Gnosticism rejected the incarnation and deity of Christ since Spirit, which was part of God who is good, could not unite with flesh, which was matter and therefore evil. Today the liberals, modernists, Jehovah's Witnesses, neo-evangelicals and countless others reject the deity of Christ. They deny the fact that He was incarnate God. However, John combats all this in

his gospel:

> In the beginning was the Word and the Word was with God and the Word was God (John 1:1).

> And the Word was made flesh, and dwelt among us ..." (John 1:14).

Then John continues his attack in his First Epistle (1:1, 2:22; 4:2-3, 5:5-6). Jesus Christ was, is, and will always be God.

2. Gnosticism also rejected the resurrection, just as many do today. However, in addition to all John says about the resurrection in his gospel and his epistle, he says something very special in 1 John 3:2:

> Behold, now are we the children of God, and it doth not yet appear what we shall be, but we know that, when He shall appear, we shall be like Him; for we shall see Him as He is.

Not only is He a *risen* Lord, He is a *returning* Lord.

3. Gnosticism rejected the Scriptures as literal. It said that the non-literal and mystical sense of the Scriptures could only be understood by a select few. Today we have the same basic thoughts not only in liberalism, modernism, and neo-orthodoxy but also in Catholicism as well. Of all the "private interpreters" the Roman Church leads them all in heresy covering every subject from false salvation and idol worship to out-and-out paganism. Catholicism says you don't need to read your Bible. The priest and the pope will tell you all you need to know. They don't want you to read the Scriptures. When Martin Luther read his Bible, he was converted to Christ. What heresy it is for a man to think he has some superior knowledge. John does away with that notion in the first verse of this epistle along with verses 3-5 in Chapter 2. We are to keep the commandments of God, for only God's Word in its simplicity can meet man's needs.

4. Gnosticism, because of the evil in the world, rejected God as the only creator. This is quite reminiscent of theistic evolution, but again in 1 John 1:1 and John 1:1-3 we have those important and foundational passages concerning Christ as the creator.

5. Gnosticism taught that knowledge is superior to virtue. Only knowledge matters. As we have seen already, that is what the humanist of today says. Man is the center of all things and

all that matters is how we advance intellectually and technologically. So, when it comes to conduct, just do what you feel like doing—do what comes naturally. Humanism is rampant today, but John says much about it. He tells us, "Don't sin" (1 John 2:1), sin is the breaking of God's law (3:4), and live like Jesus lived (2:6).

John's encouragement is to beware. There are many who have gone out into the world to deceive (2 John 7). God wants us to be knowledgeable of the truth of His Word so we will not be deceived by false doctrine (Eph. 4:14). He wants us to have nothing to do with those who would teach false doctrine even to the extent of not allowing them into our homes or giving a greeting of encouragement (2 John 10-11).

* * * * *

John's first epistle is truly an encouraging one. Are we really joyful? Are we living holy? Are we assured in our faith? Are we heeding God's warning?

CHAPTER NINE

God's Part in Communication: His Word

Thy Word have I hidden in mine heart, that I might not sin against thee (Ps. 119:11)

What is "true communication"? A simple definition of communication would be "the giving and receiving of information." There is a great lack of real communication these days. Some years ago a popular phrase to use was "the generation gap," but this "gap" was only a breakdown in communication. People seldom take the time to communicate with each other. To have "true communication," all parties involved must be "giving and receiving information."

However, more importantly we should realize that the biggest failure of man is his lack of communication with God. We are so often so busy and caught up in the world that we do not communicate with our Heavenly Father. Now, since true communication is the giving and receiving of information to and from all parties involved, then there must, therefore, be a way which

God speaks *directly* to us and a way which we speak *directly* to Him. We *do* have these direct means of communicating with God. God speaks directly to us through His Word and we communicate directly to Him through prayer. In this chapter we want to see "God's Part in Communication," that is, how He speaks directly to us through His Word.

What place should the Word of God have in our lives as believers? I would like to give you a simple outline for the way to use the Word of God in your Christian life. Wherever I go in my preaching and teaching ministry I have tried to encourage believers of the importance of God's Word in their lives. This is one of the greatest burdens in my ministry. I have already mentioned it earlier in this book, but now I want to take special note of some things here on how to use your Bible. I'm not going to give a mini-course on study methods but rather a simple outline for using God's Word.

Dear Christian, we need the Word of God in our lives. How important it is to our living! Is God's Word the controlling force in your life? Is it the most important thing to your Christian walk? Let us examine a fourfold outline for using God's Word.

I. MARK IT

First of all, we ought to *mark* God's Word. Notice Jeremiah 23:18:

> For who hath stood in the counsel of the Lord and hath perceived and heard His Word? Who hath marked His Word and heard it?

Of course, this does not mean to mark with a pencil or pen. Who has listened with a hearing ear and marked down what God says in their *mind* and *heart*? The word "mark" comes from a word in the Hebrew which means to "regard or heed." The entreaty then is to look at it, regard what it says, and heed what it says.

As we consider this in a practical way, let us realize the blessing we all have as believers to own a Bible, probably more than one. We all, especially those of us who have the blessing of living in a free country, possess one or more copies of the inspired and preserved Word of God passed down through the centuries from God to man. As we think of this, may we ask ourselves, "How often do I take the Word of God for granted?" How often do we look at it and say by our actions the way we treat it—"Well I have it, but I won't mark it or heed it"?

May I challenge you, the reader, further on how we physically treat God's Word. The Word of God, even the copies we have today, is *sacred.* Do we treat it as sacred? Do we let it gather dust on a shelf? Do we lay it on the floor? If we have a stack of books, is it on top? Do we use it for a coaster as we set a cup of coffee on it? Do we toss it onto a table or desk or the church pew? This is not "bibliolatry" (Bible worship); it is respect and reverence for what is sacred.

To further make this marking of God's Word practical for today, let us consider what a blessing it is that we cannot only possess a copy of God's Word to mark down in our *minds,* but we can also mark it on the *page.* There is nothing wrong with *reverently* underlining or shading verses and passages of Scripture. Let us take care not to do this haphazardly, but let us do it systematically—always viewing God's Word as sacred.

Still another point to ponder on marking God's Word on the page is the taking of notes during messages. Many Christians miss lasting blessing by not taking down the major points of a message along with important statements the preacher makes in his exposition. What happens most often is Christians listen to the preaching and may get an encouragement—a blessing—or learn something new, but they don't write it down and so quickly lose it. Many Christians have lost countless wealth by not having a notebook full of message notes which they can refer back to over and over and receive new blessing as they meditate upon them.

Dear Christian, are you *marking* God's Word? Are you regarding it and heeding it? "Who hath marked His Word and heard it?"

II. MEMORIZE IT

Another principle for using God's Word is to *memorize* it. Look at our text for this chapter again:

> Thy Word have I hidden in mine heart, that I might not sin against thee.

Oh, how important it is to memorize the Scriptures! It is here that I believe many Christians are greatly lacking. In addition, Scripture memorization seems to be little emphasized by preachers and pastors.

Many Bible colleges emphasize the memorizing of lengthy passages of Scripture in certain Bible classes. I remember doing this in many of my classes in my early school days. However, this practice seems quite wrong to me. You cannot force someone to memorize anything, even Scripture, and expect them to remember it the day after the exam. They must *want* to commit the Scriptures to memory. They must love God's Word so much that they *want* to hide it in their hearts.

Another danger is that often Christians decide to "start memorizing Scripture" and so they jump into it only from the perspective that it is a mental exercise. What often happens is that they soon stop doing it for one reason or another. They may have a difficult time learning the verses or they may have just gotten busy with "things."

However, the key to "hiding God's Word" in your heart is to hide it in your *heart,* not your *head.* We emphasize the mental so much that we completely leave out the spiritual. Never memorize a verse just to be memorizing. Memorize it because it speaks to you personally. It challenges you. It blesses you. It convicts you. It helps you with a problem. There are many methods today that good men have come up with for memorizing. The topical approach is popular. These may have some merit, but it seems the best way to hide God's Word in our hearts is by daily reading and meditating on His Word and committing to our hearts that which He lays upon them. If you memorize with your heart, you will soon discover that you know a lot more Scripture from memory.

The word for "hide" is a Hebrew word meaning to conceal. It is used figuratively here to mean "lay up in the heart." We often "lay up" or "put back" things which we greatly value. Many of us probably have things put away which go back to childhood or high school days—most of which are worthless but mean something to us. In addition, many Christians are caught up in the "investment craze" and are trying to make money and put back large amounts for a "rainy day." Nonetheless, how many of us are "laying up" and "putting back" God's Word in our hearts.

The things we memorize are the things which control our thoughts. Most men can quote technical things about their jobs. Many can quote statistics about favorite ball teams and sports people. Many ladies can give a favorite recipe to a friend from memory. The human mind can memorize anything it desires to commit to memory. Why, then, is it that we do not *want* to memorize the most important thing in the universe—God's Word!

Why does God implore us to "hide His Word" in our hearts? The rest of the verse explains why—"that we might not sin against thee." The only thing which can bring victory in distress, discouragement, and danger is the Word of God which we have in our hearts. When our Saviour was three times tempted by Satan, how did He combat the temptation? Not by will power, not by clever wit, but *by quoting Scripture.* The Lord Jesus defeated temptation. Three times Satan tempts and three times our Lord says, "It is written." *That* is how we have victory over temptation.

Hebrews 4:15 tell us:

> For we have not an high priest who cannot be touched with the feeling of our infirmities, but was in all points tempted like as we are, yet without sin.

In 1 John 2:16, we see there are three categories of sin, "the lust of the flesh, the lust of the eyes, and the pride of life, . . ." Jesus was tempted in all three categories. When tempted by the flesh (Matt. 4:3-4), He quotes Deuteronomy 8:13. When tempted by sight (Matt. 4:9-10), He quotes Deuteronomy 6:13. Then, when tempted by pride and self-elevation (Matt. 4:6-7), Jesus quotes Deuteronomy 6:16. He quoted the words of God and claimed victory.

However, if we look at another biblical figure, we can see what happens when we don't hide God's Word in our heart to keep us from sin. Note the temptation of Eve in Genesis 3:1-6. Eve "saw that the tree was good for food" (lust of the flesh), "it was pleasant to the eyes" (lust of the eyes), and it was "to be desired to make one wise" (pride of life). If only she would have quoted God's Word. No she didn't have the *written* Word, but she did have the *spoken* Word. She perverted what God had said. When we compare what God said in Genesis 2:16-17 with what Eve said in 3:2-3, we see a great difference. Eve left out the words "every" and "freely," thus detracting from God's grace. She also inserts "neither shall you touch it," thus making God a little narrow-minded. She then changes the phrase "surely die" to "lest ye die," thus softening God's punishment for disobedience. Oh, if only she had *quoted* God instead of *paraphrasing* God!

Christian, are you taking the time to hide His Word in your heart that you might not sin against Him? Are you allowing His Word to permeate your every thought? I do think we must be careful of too many "Christian cliches," but one I think which is worthy of note is, "God's Word will keep you from sin or sin will keep you from God's Word."

III. MEDITATE ON IT

The third principle for using God's Word is to *meditate* on it. Some years ago I heard a dear pastor preach a beautiful message on Psalm 19:14:

Let the words of my mouth, and the meditation of my heart, be acceptable in Thy sight, oh Lord, my strength, and my redeemer.

That message is always in my memory when I preach on this subject of meditation. I have many times *marked* and have *memorized* this marvelous verse and have quite often sat and *meditated* upon it.

What is meditation? The world has done much to pervert the word meditation, but let us not throw out an important spiritual exercise just because of Satan's counterfeit. The word used here comes from a Hebrew word which means, "the murmur or dull sound of a harp; hence, a style of music which is soft and subdued." A similar word is found in Joshua 1:8 and Psalm 1:2. It reflects the sighing and low sounds one makes while deep in thought. This pictures one who while deep in thought will occasionally utter a low "hmmm" as something strikes them which they never thought of before.

Therefore, real meditation is "quiet, concentrated thought." Does not the Hebrew give us a beautiful picture? As in the murmur of a harp as it softly plays, we are to sit alone and quietly ponder the Word of God.

Oh, may we not forget the words in 1 Kings 19:11-12. Elijah

has fled from Jezebel's wrath and is discouraged. God is now encouraging him:

> And he said, Go forth, and stand upon the mount before the Lord. And, behold, the Lord passed by, and a great and strong wind rent the mountains, and broke in pieces the rocks before the Lord; but the Lord was not in the wind. And after the wind an earthquake; but the Lord was not in the earthquake. And after the earthquake a fire; but the Lord was not in the fire. And after the fire *a still small voice* (emphasis mine).

Again the Hebrew sheds great light. It paints the picture that this still, small voice is a "gentle blowing" or the sound of gentle stillness. Imagine yourself alone, on top of a mountain, surrounded by perfect stillness and an occasional soft breeze upon your face. It is *there* that God speaks. He does not speak in fanfare. He does not speak in applause. He does not speak in a lightning bolt. He does not speak in the clanking cymbal and the beating drum. He does not speak through some emotional outburst. He speaks in *a still, small voice.*

The question which we must ask ourselves is, "Are we listening to that still, small voice?" How often do we sit down and take just one verse, one phrase, or even one word and meditate upon it? This is when God is going to give us the greatest blessings. It is when we get alone with God and His Word and quietly ponder what He says that we find ourselves quietly uttering, "hmmm, I never saw that before. Oh, how marvelous that truth is. Thank you, Lord, for letting me see it."

There is such a great lack of meditation upon God's Word these days among Christians. We can devour a newspaper, a news magazine, various periodicals, and novels, as well as watch television and listen to the radio or stereo, and we can completely engulf ourselves in a job or hobby. All of these are fine as long as they are controlled, but if these are coming between us and God or taking away from the time we should be in His Word than they, according to Hebrews 12:1, have become "weights":

> Wherefore, seeing we also are compassed about with so great a cloud of witnesses, let us lay aside every weight, and the sin which doth so easily beset us, and let us run with patience the race that is set before us.

A "weight" is something which in itself is *not* sinful. It is something which has *become* sinful in our lives because we give it a place over the things of God. There's nothing in the rules of track and field that says a runner can't wear lead boots in the race if he so desires. However, those boots are going to cause him to lose the race and receive no reward. Likewise, there may be some things in our lives which we should either bring under control or get rid of entirely.

May we note also one word in our text, "acceptable." David's desire here is that the words he says and the very meditations he has be "well-pleasing" to God. We can meditate on *anything.* The challenge David puts to us is that what we meditate upon should be to the furtherance of our spiritual growth.

Another thought which always comes to mind when meditating on this verse is that these words of David *flow from his heart.* It is here we see the great connection between *memorization* and *meditation.* When we understand the fact that the Psalms were poems which were put to music, it enlightens us to the heart of David. Can we not imagine David sitting and playing his harp as words of praise and adoration of God flowed from his heart? The music and the words were a part of David. They came from him because they permeated his being.

Oh, how marvelous it would be if every born again child of God had the heart of David! How wonderful it would be if the words of our mouths and the meditations of our hearts were acceptable in God's sight. May we all really meditate on God's Word. May we be willing to get alone, sit down, and block out everything around us and ponder His Word, ponder His majesty and holiness, ponder who He is, what He has done, what He is doing, and what He is going to do.

Our Lord speaks in "a still, small voice." Many cannot hear Him because they are too busy, moving too fast, and making too much noise. If we do not make the time to get alone with God and listen, we are not only going to miss great blessings but are going to answer for it and possibly suffer for it in this present life. Dear Christian, get alone with God everyday. Take the time to *meditate* on His Word.

O, Lord, I desire every day to get alone with Thee;
To meditate upon Thy Word, Thy face to clearly see.

IV. MASTER IT

The final principle we see for using God's Word is to *master* it as we allow it to master us. Note our main text again:

Thy Word have I hidden in mine heart that I might not sin against thee.

In order for us to be able to "hide" God's Word we must first of all "have it." We cannot hide, lay up, store, or put back that which we do not possess. Therefore, we must "master the Word of God," that is, *we must have a working knowledge and a strategic grasp of God's Word.*

Now what does this "working knowledge and strategic grasp" mean? By this, I mean that we must have an overall view of what the Bible is about, its theme and purpose, its dispensational structure, its cardinal doctrines, and those foundational truths that God wants us to have engrained and engrafted in our hearts and lives. I again encourage you, the reader, to the second appendix for some recommended reading which will aid you in acquiring that strategic grasp. Countless Christians these days are erring greatly because they do not have this working knowledge. Christianity today needs less laziness and more sincere love for God's Word. The need today is for God's people to love His Word more than anything else in their lives and to be diligent students of it.

I must at this point say there is a great tragedy among preachers today. Many of them, it is sad to say, are shirking their first responsibility as a man of God, which is, the preaching of the Word of God. Often they are so busy with calling on people, and other "ministerial duties," that they do not prepare adequately for the preaching ministry, and their preaching shows it. Many sermons and Bible lessons these days are topical and often deal with current events and issues, rather than the clear exposition of God's truth. A pastor who is not spending a certain number of hours each day in study for the preaching and teaching ministry is greatly erring from his divinely ordained responsibility. It is not the pastor's job to "win the goats," but it is his job to "feed the sheep." Yes, he must do many other things, but he must first and foremost "preach the Word" (2 Tim. 4:2).

Coming back to the thought that every Christian must have "a strategic grasp of the Scriptures" we see that only then will we have victory, growth, and be an effective witness for Christ.

Let us ponder together three questions from your point of view:

1. "How much of the Word of God do I *know*?" Do I understand those basic doctrines which are so vital to the Christian faith? Can I give just simple and basic explanations to justification, sanctification, adoption, dispensations, and law and grace? The question I must ask myself is, "How can I possibly expect to be an effective Christian if I do not have a grasp of His Word?"

2. "Do I know *what* I believe?" In addition to the major doctrines of the Bible, do I know the principles for living, for growth, and for conduct?

3. "Do I know *why* I believe what I believe?" When many Christians are asked why they believe a certain thing, the answer is, "Well, that's what my pastor believes." This may be true, and that pastor may be right, but that is a very poor reason for belief. Believe something because you have studied it.

Now, does all this mean that God wants all of us to be theologians? No, but He wants us to know His Word. Few Christians are going to know Hebrew and Greek. Most of us in America only speak the American brand of English. Few Christians will ever have systematic theology or other seminary training. However, we all can still have this "strategic grasp." As we have seen in an earlier chapter, this is why God directed Peter to write:

> But grow in grace and in the knowledge of our Lord and Saviour, Jesus Christ (2 Peter 3:18).

One of the most important verses for *every* Christian is found in 2 Timothy 2:15. While this is written directly to a pastor showing his responsibility, it still has an application to every believer:

> Be diligent to present yourself approved unto God as a workman who does not need to be ashamed, handling accurately the Word of Truth (NASV).

Without getting too deep into this verse, let us briefly see the import of this verse in the believer's life.

The King James Version uses the word "study" which in 1611 meant "diligent" as the Greek indicates. Every believer should have an eagerness and diligence toward God's Word. As we noted in Chapter 4, "to show" is the same word in the Greek as the words "to present" in Romans 12:1. The emphasis here is on our complete dedication to God's Word and will. "Not ashamed" shows us a twofold truth. When we are diligent and love God's Word we will not be ashamed of ourselves when we stand before the Lord at the Judgment Seat of Christ. Every believer should use the Word of God by "rightly dividing" or "cutting straight" or "handling accurately" or "setting it forth without distortion."

Obviously, all of this takes *work*. That is why Paul uses the term "workman" or laborer. However, the question is, per week, do we devote seconds, minutes, or hours to the *marking, memorizing, meditating,* and *mastery* of God's Word?

As we draw this chapter to a close, may we once again touch on our usage of the Word of God. There are really only three basic things which will bring about the *mastery* of the Word.

1. Attendance of a local church where there is the deep, expository preaching of the Word. This is the primary way God's people are going to grow. It is the pastor's responsibility to spend the majority of his time in the Word so that he may be prepared to teach his people. It then is the people's responsibility to attend God's house, listen to the Word, and apply it to their lives.

2. The daily reading of the Scriptures. This seems obvious, but it needs to be emphasized over and over. There are many "programs" for reading through the Bible, but there is some danger in these. They can be *very* good, but they can also be equally bad. Many Christians get into one of these programs and read every day, but sometimes their reading becomes so mechanical that they are reading just to fulfill the daily requirement. Quite often a shorter portion of Scripture is going to be of much greater value than a longer one. You may not "read the Bible through in a year," but you will be a deeper Christian if you take the extra time. Never allow a *plan* to overshadow the *purpose.*

Coupled with this daily reading is the reading of "devotional books" or daily readings. There are many good ones out today. These can *supplement* your Bible reading, but they must never replace it.

3. The reading of Christian books. I told the story in an earlier chapter of the bookstore owner who told me that if it wasn't for the Jehovah's Witnesses in that city, he could not stay in business. It is tragic indeed that Christians do not buy and read books. This, of course, may not refer to you, for you are obviously reading right now. However, we can never get enough of God's Word. It is vital that Christians *read* and encourage *other* Christians to read the books which have blessed their hearts.

Why is it that Christians don't read more than they do? The answer I believe goes back to what we noticed in *meditation—* too many other things which "crowd out" the Word of God. In my own life I have to be very careful that my interest in history and my reading of history do not crowd out God's Word. If there is *anything* in our lives which keeps us from the Book, it is sin. What place do we give God's Word in our lives?

* * * * *

Dear fellow Christian, what place do you give the Word of God in your life? Is it just something you pick up on the way to church so you can follow along as the preacher reads? Or, is it the very force in your life: your guide and your master?

In one of the greatest revivals in biblical history we find a great admonition. In Nehemiah 8:1 to 10:39 we have recorded the great revival which took place under Ezra. The words we see spoken by the people to Ezra were: "Bring the Book." What mattered most was the reading of the Word of God and the explanation of it by God's man. They never knew the blessing we know of having the finished Word which we may read on our own. Oh, that we would exercise that marvelous blessing! Oh, may we *mark* it, *memorize* it, *meditate* upon it, and *master* it, for only when we do will it "master us."

May I close this chapter with something abundantly practical? I would like to give a twofold challenge. May you, the reader, pray about each and see if God would have you do them.

1. Would you be willing to covenant with God to mark out a definite period of time, say a week, and spend the time that you

normally spend watching television, reading secular literature, or other similar activities, and spend it marking, memorizing, and especially meditating upon God's Word? I believe that at the end of that time you will find that you have not only grown but that also your whole schedule will be changed in such a way that God's Word has a new place of prominence.

2. Would you also make a covenant with God that during the next year you will read at least four to six Christian books? These should not be just "Christian novels," but personal growth books like those given in the second appendix of this book. Again, I think you will find that your life will grow in marvelous ways.

Does God's Word have first place?

CHAPTER TEN

Our Part in Communication: Prayer

As we continue our thoughts on communication, let us meditate on one verse. Luke 18:1 reads:

And he spoke a parable unto this end, that men ought always to pray, and not to faint.

In the last chapter we looked at what true communication is and, that in order to have it, all parties involved must be "giving and receiving information." We saw there that God has a *direct* way to speak to us which is His Word. To balance out this communication, we will now look at how we can directly speak to God which is through prayer.

There have been many books written on this subject of prayer, indeed too many, for many of them are too shallow even to the point of ignorance. However, no book on the Christian life would be complete unless prayer was emphasized. I want to look first at prayer *foundationally*, that is, exactly what prayer *is*. In the first part of our study we will see that prayer is far more than what we sometimes think it to be. *True prayer* is so far beyond what we usually think of prayer, that before the chapter is complete some may wonder if they have ever really prayed. Then, we want to look at prayer *functionally,* that is, some suggestions for putting true prayer into practice.

I. THE FOUNDATIONS OF PRAYER

By the term "foundations of prayer" I mean, what prayer is. There are seven Greek words which are translated "prayer" in the New Testament. Four of the seven are used in one verse. 1 Timothy 2:1:

> I exhort, therefore, that first of all supplications, prayers, inter-cessions, and giving of thanks, be made by all men.

These words are those which are used most often concerning prayer. The first word is the word "supplications." The Greek word used here carries the idea of a request *and* stresses the sense of need in the request. The word shows sincerity, earnestness, and intenseness, but it does *not* mean to beg and plead with God as some would teach. Nowhere does the Bible teach us to beg and plead. It teaches us to ask according to God's will as we will point out again later.

The next word Paul uses is "prayers," which is the general word used for prayer in the New Testament. The Greek *proseuché* indicates the making known a wish or desire. The next word, "intercessions," means to converse in a familiar way in order to plead the case of someone else. The last word is "thanksgiving," which in the Greek is *eucharistia.* Roman Catholicism has built a completely false doctrine upon the word. Their "Holy Eucharist" teaches that salvation comes by literally partaking of the actual body and blood of Jesus. Every Catholic mass crucifies Christ again. However, the real significance of the word lies in the fact that the root *charis* is the common word for "grace" and "graciousness," and the prefix *eu* is an adverb meaning "well" or "good." Therefore, *eucharistia* is the act of giving thanks or "conversation marked by the gentle cheerfulness of a grateful heart."

There are three other words which occur only occasionally in the New Testament. One of them is *euché*, meaning a vow or wish. Another is *aitéma* meaning a request or petition. One other is *hikētria* which refers to a supplication. In the words of a great Greek scholar of years past, Richard Trench, these seven Greek words for prayer are "not different kinds of prayer, but different aspects of prayer" (*Synonyms of the New Testament*). Each one tells us something about prayer, something of its depths.

However, with all this in mind, what *is* prayer? What does it really mean to pray? Prayer is much more than just offering petitions or asking God for things. I read a book many years ago that defined prayer as "asking and receiving." How many parents would enjoy having children who only spoke to them when they wanted something? Nonetheless, this is how many people view prayer.

Prayer is definitely more than just offering petitions. It is more than making a sincere, earnest, and intense request. It is even more than giving thanks. We may define true prayer this way: *Prayer is constant communion with God.* I ask you, the reader, to stop right now and engrain this thought in your mind and heart, "prayer is constant communion with God."

To help understand this definition, it is vital that we make a contrast between two words. Often when we say "prayer," we are really referring to "prayers." When we say we are going to a "prayer meeting," we really should say we are going to have a "prayers meeting." The reason for this distinction is that "prayers" are those specific times when we bring our needs and burdens to God. However, "prayer" is a constant, day-by-day, minute-by-minute communion with God. Prayer is not when we just come before God and ask of Him, or have a conversation with Him, but the true reality of prayer is a constant, second-by-second *communion* with Almighty God. If we can just engrain this thought in our hearts, oh, how it will deepen our lives!

Another way of expressing this truth is that often preachers, speak of either being *in* fellowship with God or *out of* fellowship with God. In like manner, we are either communing with God or we're not communing with God. One other way I have heard this expressed is most blessed, "Prayer is living our lives in God-consciousness." The great challenge here is that every moment we live we should be conscious of the fact that God is with us, beside us, and in us. Our whole life should be lived with a consciousness of God's presence.

Let us note three things which our text says about prayer.

A. The Constantness of Prayer

First, our text says we are to *"always* pray." Luke tells us there should always be constant prayer within us. There should be moment-by-moment prayer taking place. This parallels exactly with what Paul tells us in 1 Thessalonians 5:17:

Pray without ceasing.

There is not one of us who can, "without ceasing," constantly, every moment of every day, be saying "prayers" to God. That is not possible. Therefore, Paul and Luke must be referring to something else. Indeed they are, for "prayers" are those *specific* times while "prayer" is *constant* communion.

A most marvelous verse is found in Colossians 3:2:

Set your affection on things above, not on things on the earth.

The Christian is to seek the upper things. The Christian is to set his or her mind and heart on the things of heaven, not on the things this world can offer. Based upon this verse that great expositor G. Campbell Morgan wrote: "This is the simple meaning of prayer. Reaching forward, wishing forward, desiring forward, seeking the upper, the higher, the nobler."

What a challenge! To really be praying, that is, to really be constantly communing with God, we must be seeking the higher and the nobler things. Many think that if they are faithful to midweek prayer meeting or if they pray before they eat or if they pray before going to sleep, then they are a "praying Christian." However, the question is not whether or not we offer prayers, but rather are we praying Christians? Do we have the constant communion with God? The way to know that we are praying Christians, that is, to know that we are constantly communing with God, we must examine our lives and see if we are seeking the higher and nobler things. Our affection will be set on the things of heaven, not on the things of this world. We will truly be walking with Him.

B. The Comfort of Prayer

Not only does Jesus tell us to *always* pray, but He then tells

us to always pray and *not faint.* There is in this constant communion a marvelous comfort. I look at this and it is such a thrill
to my own heart! Our Lord knows that the Christian life is difficult because He encourages us not to faint. By fainting, our
Lord means to lose heart or get discouraged and so He says, "I
want you to pray and not be discouraged, though I know that
living this way is hard."

The word "faint" carries the idea of being paralyzed, weak,
worthless, beaten and totally broken. Have you ever felt
broken, weak, and even paralyzed, unable to move spiritually?
Have you ever felt really downtrodden and not really knowing
why? The reason is that "praying" and "fainting" are *opposites.*
When you are praying you cannot faint, but when you faint it
is because you are not praying. Oh, when you are really communing with God you won't faint. No matter what the situation
may be, you will not be discouraged if you are communing with
God.

It seems Isaiah knew this, for in Isaiah 40:31 he tells us:

> But they that wait upon the Lord shall renew their strength;
> they shall mount up with wings like eagles; they shall run, and not
> be weary; and they shall walk, and not faint.

We looked at this verse back in Chapter 6, but it is worth looking at again in a different context. That phrase "they that wait
upon the Lord" can only be true when we are really praying. To
wait upon God is to put His will first. To wait upon God is to
live patiently. To wait upon God is to be in constant communion with Him.

So, Isaiah tells us that they who wait, they who pray, will
have their strength renewed in three stages. First, God is our
strength during the easy times. When everything is going good,
we "shall mount up with wings as eagles." It is during these
times we must take care to remember that it is His strength that
keeps us going. Second, God renews our strength in the everyday problems and difficulties of life. We are no longer soaring
high, but we can still "run and not be weary." However, the
third stage is when the serious problems come—the tragedies of
life. It is at this point that His strength is ever present and even
though we may not be "soaring" or even "running," we will still
be able to *walk and not faint.*

Oh, our Lord is always present with His strength. Isaiah understood the value of real prayer, the value of real communion with God. Oh, that we would also understand. When we are in constant communion with God, when we get our eyes off of this world, and set our affections on the things of God, we will then mount up with wings as eagles, we'll run and not be weary, and we will walk and not faint. What could be greater than that?

C. The Command of Prayer

Let us take all of this one step further. Jesus not only tells us to *always* pray and to pray and *not faint,* but He also commands us that we *ought* to pray. Prayer is not only a "privilege" (and what a marvelous privilege it is), but it is also a "duty." We *ought* to pray. We *must* pray. We must *always* pray. We must always pray and *not faint.*

What a tragedy we see today in that Christians do not pray. This is why we have a great lack of power in our churches and in our lives. This is why we no longer influence society and the people with whom we come in contact every day. This is why we do not see faithfulness and consistency in our lives. All of this simply because we do not pray. Many of us are "quick-on-the draw" when it comes to saying "prayers," but are not really "praying Christians." What a privilege it is to pray, but, oh, what a duty it is as well.

* * * * *

Drawing all this together, we recall our definition of true prayer: "constant communion with God" or as we also noted, "living our lives in God consciousness." When we are living every moment conscious of the God we serve and constantly communing with Him, we will not faint. We will be powerful, we will be faithful, we will be fruitful, we will be victorious, and we will know real joy and peace.

I do prayerfully hope that you, the reader, understand what true prayer is. It is more than just "prayers." Prayers *are* important. It is vital that we take the time to sit down in concentrated conversation with God through prayers bringing specific praises, thanksgivings, examinations, intercessions, and petitions to Him. However, true prayer is a constant moment-by-moment living.

II. THE FUNCTIONS OF PRAYER

As we noted earlier all the Greek words translated "prayer" do not denote different *kinds* of prayer but different *aspects* of prayer. Each one shows a different manifestation of the one reality. In the remainder of the chapter we want to examine the functions of prayer or the "fivefold pattern of prayer," as told to us by the Lord Jesus in Matthew 6:9-13.

Up until now we have emphasized that prayer is constant communion with God. This should always be kept in mind. However, we now need to look with equal depth into the importance of "prayers" and realize the necessity of our *conversation* with God as well as our *communion* with God. How important it is that Christians today realize the necessity of their prayers. We have weak churches because we have weak Christians. We have weak Christians because they don't pray. Many do not take the time each day to concentrate in praying. God has given some principles in His Word for praying correctly and it is important that we pray as God has outlined. May we take careful note of "The Model Prayer" in Matthew 6:

> After this manner, therefore, pray ye: Our Father, who art in heaven, Hallowed by thy name. Thy kingdom come. Thy will be done in earth, as it is in heaven. Give us this day our daily bread. And forgive us our debts, as we forgive our debtors. And lead us not into temptation, but deliver us from evil. For thine is the kingdom, and the power, and the glory, forever. Amen.

Let it be clear that this is not what many call the "Lord's Prayer." It is not the Lord's Prayer, He never prayed this prayer. In fact, He could *not* pray this prayer because He never sinned, so He could not ask for forgiveness. It was given to the disciples as a *model,* a basic outline of what their prayers should contain.

The words, "After this manner, therefore, pray ye," clearly show that this is not a prayer to be prayed but a model to be followed. We see many churches today quoting this prayer in a worship service, but this is not its intended purpose at all. In fact, in all of the New Testament we do not have a single record of a word-for-word prayer by anyone except the *real* Lord's prayer in John 17. Here is a special high-priestly intercessory prayer offered by the Lord Jesus Christ, God in the flesh, which we could never pray. The Lord's prayer is just that—the prayer that only the Lord Jesus could pray. However, the model prayer is a "skeleton," a foundation on which we build our prayers.

Let us look at this model prayer and see a fivefold pattern which should be a part of our prayers *and* prayer. These are not only guidelines for our *conversation* with God but also our *communion* with God as well.

A. Praise

"Our Father, who are in heaven, Hallowed be thy name." How important it is that we praise and worship our God. It is essential that prayer begin *with* and be permeated *by* praise and worship. There are some four hundred instances in the Scriptures where the words "praise" and "worship" are used toward God. May we stop and ponder the fact that when we pray we actually come into the presence of God. Think of it! We come in the very presence of God, the God who made the universe and all that is in it.

One of the greatest tragedies in our churches today is a lack of *worship.* There are many who claim to be evangelical or fundamental, but they blaspheme God's house with their promotionalism and sideshow methods. Still others feel that other aspects of Christian service are more important than worship. However, God tells us that our first and foremost responsibility as believers is to worship. The main reason the church was instituted was for believers to have a place to meet for worship, fellowship, and teaching.

One of the most blessed passages on worship is Psalm 95. Note verse 6:

> Oh, come, let us worship and bow down; let us kneel before the
> Lord our maker.

The Hebrew word used here for worship is *shachah,* and oh, how beautiful that word is! It is used some ninety times to show worship of God. Sixteen of these occurrences are in the Psalms. It means, "to bow down; to prostrate one's self before."

When we really meditate upon this word we see it shows not only the *purpose* of worship, which is to decrease self and increase God, but it also shows the *position* of true worship which is on our faces before Him.

Let us also see that this is not just an Old Testament teaching. A similar Greek word is used in the New Testament. The word is *proskuneō*, from whence we get the English word "prostrate." It is used some fifty times to show worship of God. The wise men came to worship the Christ child (Matt. 2:2, 11). In response to Satan's temptation Jesus said, "Thou shalt worship the Lord, thy God, and Him only shalt thou serve" (Matt. 4:10). Paul declared that men have "exchanged the truth of God for a lie and worshiped and served the creature more than the creator . . ." (Rom. 1:25). Paul also shows that when a man is convicted of his sin and comes to Christ, then "the secrets of his heart are made manifest: and so falling down on his face he will worship God . . ." (1 Cor. 14:24-25).

However, of special note is Paul's words in Acts 24:14. Paul is before the governor Felix and replies:

> But this I confess unto thee that, after the way which they call heresy, so worship I the God of my fathers, believing all things which are written in the law and in the prophets.

Paul knew what worship is even though others accused him of heresy. Likewise, today there are those who say worship is "formalism" or "liberalism." They see nothing wrong with loud talking or whispering in the sanctuary before the service begins. They see nothing wrong with allowing children to run in God's house. They see nothing wrong with all the unnecessary, silly, and even worldly "announcements" that are so often given in the service. They see nothing wrong with shallow songs they sing which they say are better and more "in tune with the times" than the old hymns of worship.

However, may we say all this is most abominable. There is indeed a great danger in dead orthodoxy and liturgy. However, *while there is a false piety to be avoided, there is a true dignity to be preserved.* God demands that we come to worship Him in prayerful silence and meditation and that all the things we do in our worship services *must* be truly worship. God doesn't demand anything less from us than He did from those recorded in

His Word. If we really think about it, we will discover that padded pews and other comforts have replaced the effort that real worship demands. Are we coming before God on our faces and really worshiping Him?

Oh, Lord, my God, my Saviour,
Thou art always the same.
May I fall on my face in reverence
To worship and praise Thy name.

Space prohibits a deeper investigation of this subject. I must leave it for another volume. However, we must see that our prayer life must be permeated by praise and worship. Our *attitudes* in this will dictate our *actions*. If Christians are worshiping in their everyday walk and in their specific times of prayer, then our churches are also going to be worshiping as God intends. "Our Father who art in heaven, Hallowed be thy name." Oh, may we constantly see His holiness, His majesty, His power. How marvelous that old hymn that says:

O worship the King, all glorious above.
O gratefully sing His wonderful love.
Our Shield and Defender, the Ancient of days,
Pavillioned in splendour, and girded with praise.

B. Thanksgiving

Thanksgiving is always coupled with praise and worship in God's Word. "Our Father, who art in heaven, Hallowed be thy name." How could we ever worship Him without showering Him with thanks? Or, how could we ever thank Him without reverently worshiping Him? Again we notice Psalm 95, it shows this coupling of worship and thanksgiving. Note verse 2:

Let us come before His presence with thanksgiving, and make a joyful noise unto Him with psalms.

We then notice Paul's teaching in Philippians 4:6:

Be anxious for nothing, but in everything by prayer and supplication, with thanksgiving, let your requests be made known unto God.

Dear Christian, if we would sit down and meditate upon all that God has given us and thank Him for every minute detail, we could pray for hours on end, never saying anything but

"Thank You, Lord." We teach our children to say thank you when someone gives them something, but, oh, how often we take for granted what God has given. Whatever God gives us, which is everything, we "take it and run" without ever stopping to thank Him. When Jesus healed the ten lepers in Luke 17:11-19 only one of them came back to thank Him. Can we imagine that? How could those nine others be so ungrateful? However, the human heart by nature is unthankful, and I really wonder if this incident is implying that only 10 percent of Christians ever really take the time to thank God for *all* that He has done. Oh, may we take the time!

C. Self-Examination

The "model prayer" also instructs us to self-examination. Verses 12 and 13 read, "forgive us our debts," and "deliver us from evil." There is here the attitude of self-examination which parallels the teaching of 2 Corinthians 13:5:

> Examine yourselves, whether you are in the faith; prove yourselves.

We are to examine ourselves in the light of God's Word to see if we match up with its standards, to see if we are reflecting Christ in our lives. Whether it is in our constant communion or whether it is in those specific times of prayers, we need to be examining our hearts and lives every moment of the day. God cannot bless if there is sin in the life. Sin is a hindrance to prayer. It breaks fellowship. It affects how God answers our prayers. We must always be examining ourselves to see if we are in the faith, that is, to see that we are *living* the faith. When we examine our lives and find sin present, it is necessary that we confess it according to 1 John 1:9 as we examined in Chapter 8.

D. Intercession

The fourth basic function of prayer is intercession. Jesus tells us this in the words of verse 12, "forgive us our debts as we forgive our debtors." Throughout God's Word we see intercessory prayer, coming before the throne of grace on the behalf of others.

I'm constantly impressed by the prayer life of the Apostle

Paul. Oh, the love he had for others as time and again he wrote, "I make mention of you always in my prayers" (Rom. 1:9, Eph. 1:16, 1 Thess. 1:2, and so forth). He was *constantly* praying for others. This shows that when a need arose in someone's life Paul prayed about it then. Quite often we today fail in this. We hear someone ask for prayer and we say, "Oh, I'll pray for you," or, "I'll pray about that need" and we *never* do. We forget. A practical way to cure this is the moment someone asks for prayer, pray right *then* in your mind and heart for that need. Don't put it off. Do it then. You may also want to write it down so you can pray later, but don't fail to pray immediately. You will find that this principle is an outworking of our constant communion.

May we emphasize how important it is to pray for others. We are often so caught up with ourselves, our wants and needs, that we never think of the needs of those around us. Every Christian ought to have specific people that he prays for and even a prayer list to remind him of these people and their needs. As we noted at the beginning of this chapter, let us look again at 1 Timothy 2:1:

> I exhort, therefore, that first of all, supplications, prayers, intercessions, and giving thanks be made for all men.

Christians who are interceding for others will find their own lives will be stronger, the Christians they are praying for will be stronger, and their church will be stronger.

E. Petition

The last things we should pray for are our own petitions. There is much that should come first, but may we thank God for the privilege of petition. How marvelous it is to know that we can come before Him with our needs and desires and ask Him to provide. Jesus' instruction was, "give us this day our daily bread." There is much we could say about this, but space only allows a short discussion. Let us ponder just a few of the admonitions on prayer in Scripture.

1. "Ye have not because ye ask not" (James 4:3). James is here speaking to self-sufficient Christians who thought they could provide for their own needs by their own means. As we saw in our chapters on worldliness these believers were con-

cerned only with wealth and prosperity through their own labor. However, James says, "Ask God." We get so busy and so caught up in the world that we forget that "God will supply all our needs according to His riches in glory by Christ Jesus" (Phil. 4:19). We must ask God for our needs, for if we do not ask, He will not give.

2. "Ye have not because ye ask amiss" (James 4:3). James now says that we often do not receive what we ask for because we ask for them with the wrong motive. We spoke of this in our study of worldliness (Chapter 5), but it is worth repeating. When we ask God for something, let us always ask ourselves why we want it. Many of us want a lot of things we do not need, but we need a lot of things we do not want and this carries over into our prayers. Do we *need* that for which we are asking? Is it going to further our Christian growth? Is it going to honor God? Will that thing ever take me away from God's Word or God's house and take up too much of my time? Let us note again Colossians 3:2:

> Set your affection on things above, not on things on the earth.

This does not mean we can never ask for things for personal enjoyment, but it does mean that our *affection* must be on spiritual things and that temporal things must never be allowed to overshadow spiritual things.

3. "If we ask anything according to his will, he heareth us" (1 John 5:14). We *must* pray according to the will of God. I have often heard people teach that we don't have to say in our prayers, "Lord, I ask for this certain thing, if it be your will." However, this is *exactly* how we should pray. God knows our needs better than we do. In fact, this is the very center of "the model prayer"—"Thy will be done." Our whole life should be lived according to the will of God. This is what real dedication is, our whole life turned completely over to divine control.

God will always answer prayer in the believer's life. Simply put, He will either—a) answer directly, that is, give us that which we ask; b) answer indirectly, that is, give us something different than what we ask, which He knows to be better for us; or c) delay His answer because of a hindrance in our lives or to just make us lean upon Him even more. Some take these three principles and say God either says "yes," "no," or "wait awhile." Though not totally accurate, they give the basic idea. The main point is that just like we do not ignore our children when they speak to us, neither does God ignore us when we pray. He always answers.

While God always answers us *when* we pray, *how* we pray will dictate how God answers. All the principles we have looked at are given so we can "pray intelligently." Many Christians do not pray intelligently. Now even when we unknowingly pray incorrectly, God still answers since the Holy Spirit "also helps our infirmities; for we know not what we should pray for as we ought; but the Spirit Himself maketh intercession for us with groanings which cannot be uttered" (Rom. 8:26). However, the more we study prayer and the more intelligently we pray, then the more effective our prayer will be and the more pleased we will make Him. And, possibly, the most important principle of all is that *we must pray according to the will of God.*

4. "Whatever ye ask in my name, that will I do, that the Father may be glorified in the Son" (John 14:13). Here we see the necessity of praying in Jesus' name. We ask all things in His name. Why? Because it is only through Him that we have anything. It is only through Him that we have access to the Father. We should close our prayers in Jesus' name, for this will show that all our requests are based upon His power.

There is a "method of prayer" which has grown popular in recent years called "conversational prayer." It is used in groups and encourages each person to just pray out loud for one or two things and so on until someone then closes. However, this is not the pattern God wants. Prayer has form to it and this method takes away that form. Each person is only making a specific petition, intercession, or other point and is, therefore, not complete in their prayer. What's even more noticeable in this "method" is that no one, except maybe the last person, prays in Jesus' name. God has given us a pattern of prayer and no man can ever improve upon it.

* * * * *

I would like to close this chapter with a few words on "fasting," unfortunately only a few. However, I feel our examination of prayer would be incomplete without it. Fasting is, "the abstinence from all physical and natural drives for a spiritual purpose." Often we think of fasting as not eating, but fasting also speaks of abstaining from other physical drives such as sleep, recreation, social contact, or even sexual activity. Of course, there is no implication that this abstinence is for a great length of time, but it is rather "on occasion" as God leads.

There are those today who teach that every Christian ought to fast at least once a week. There is also the teaching that we should set aside certain days when we fast. Some preachers even choose a certain day and call it "a day of prayer and fasting." However, none of this is taught in the Scriptures. The most important principle of fasting is taught by our Lord Jesus in the same passage where we find "the model prayer." The principle we find there is that *fasting is between you and God.* No one else is to know about it. Note Matthew 6:16-18:

> Moreover, when ye fast, be not as the hypocrites, of a sad countenance; for they disfigure their faces, that they may appear unto men to fast. Verily I say unto you, they have their reward. But thou, when thou fastest, anoint thine head, and wash thy face, that thou appear not unto men to fast, but unto thy Father, who is in secret; and thy Father, who seeth in secret, shall reward thee openly.

The Pharisees were always trying to impress everyone around them at how "spiritual" they were, so they always prayed in public and made it known to everyone around them that they were fasting. Now, public prayer is good and necessary as it is taught in God's Word, for we see many examples of it in the Scriptures. However, as we study Matthew 6:5-6, we see that the Pharisees only wanted to be seen of men and they never got alone with God. The same was true in their fasting. They wanted people to see them and say, "Oh, look at how much he sacrifices for God. How spiritual he must be."

However, God's guideline for fasting is that it is between God and the believer. It is not for others to know about or anyone to regulate. Fasting is spontaneous. It occurs at times when we are so involved in prayer, Bible study, or other spiritual activity, that we take no thought for any physical needs or drives. Because we are with God, food, sleep, or other physical needs are temporarily neglected for a higher purpose.

The question many may ask at this point is, "Is fasting necessary for the Christian?" May we answer this by a simple yes and an explanation. Every Christian should experience times when they are so involved with the Lord that they take no thought of physical needs. Our Lord not only speaks of it here, but He also teaches it in Matthew 9:14-15 that when He was gone from the earth, then there would be times for fasting in remembrance and communion. Paul encouraged fasting. Meditate upon his words in 1 Corinthians 7:5; 2 Corinthians 6:5; and 11:27. The Early Church often fasted before making major decisions such as in Acts 13:2-3 as the church at Antioch prayed and fasted before sending Paul and Barnabas on the first missionary tour. I can picture a whole group of believers as they went to prayer about this and thought of nothing else until they had the perfect peace of knowing God's will.

Yes, fasting is for Christians today and God wants them to commune with Him and at times fast in accordance with His guidelines.

*   *   *   *   *

May I close with this. This chapter is of great importance in every believer's life for three reasons: 1) To round out our communication with God. It draws together what we saw in the last chapter with what we have seen in this one. We need God's Word in our lives that God can speak directly to us and we need prayer that we may speak directly to Him. 2) To help us pray intelligently. As we said, many do not pray intelligently. May we think about *what* we pray for, *who* we pray for, and *how* we pray for it. I would like to recommend a marvelous little book on prayer by Lehman Strauss, *Sense and Nonsense About Prayer.* It is most practical and blessed. 3) To show that prayer is infinitely larger than we realize.

Dear Christian, are you a praying Christian? Do you have a "prayer life" *and* a "prayers life"?

Afterword

So, is dedication important? By now we certainly must say, "It is everything!" In this one word is the whole which itself is made up of many parts. Those many parts, however, can be reduced to those three basic features: *presentation, separation,* and *transformation.*

To be presented takes a once-for-all decision to give our lives over to divine control. To be separate we must not have a tender affection for this world system. And, to be continually transformed, we must be constantly renewing our minds with God's Word and God's presence. Perhaps we can sum it all up with the following.

The Essence of Dedication

Oh, Lord, may I present my body,
once-and-for-all to you;
may I set aside myself,
and allow your Spirit to renew.

Oh Lord, may I separate myself
from what the world says is dear;
may I realize that all it gives
is worry, and pain, and fear.

Oh Lord, may I always desire
the transforming of my mind;
may I always draw nearer to you
and leave everything else behind.

* * * * *

Appendix I
The Security of the Believer

In Chapter 8, we touched briefly on the assurance of salvation and the security of the believer. I think it best if we add to what was said there. There are many dear Christians today who reject this doctrine on the grounds that it gives a "license to sin." Well, we shall come back to this. However, what is truly necessary is the fact that we need to see that God's Word teaches the security of the believer. God tells us that when we are *truly* saved, we will never be lost again.

The reason this is so important is because the weakest Christians I know are the ones who reject this doctrine. It is a fact that those who reject the security of the believer are the most "up and down" and inconsistent Christians in the Body of Christ. I'm not being derogatory in saying this, but rather I am saying this because of concern for the spiritual growth of Christians. There is no way someone can grow deeper *in* Christ if they don't know from one moment to the next if they *are* in Christ.

I do pray these extra pages will help you or someone else who is struggling in this area. Because of the large amount of Scripture used here, and for the sake of space, references will not be quoted entirely. The reader is urged to follow the Scriptures carefully in his Bible. There are some points repeated here that were in Chapter 8, but this was necessary for the sake of continuity.

There are at least twelve scriptural proofs for the security of the believer. I'm sure one could find more, but we will consider just these.

1. The term "eternal life." Such well-known verses as John 3:15-16, 36; 4:14; 5:24; 6:27; and others all use the term "eternal life" (or "everlasting life" as in some verses in the King James Version). The Greek word used in each is *aiōnios* which is a word which simply means "indeterminate as to duration; eternal; everlasting." May we observe, in passing, there are those who make a great deal about there being a difference between

"eternal life" and "everlasting life." They say the former means life which has no beginning and will have no end; while the latter means life which has a beginning but will have no end. This is fanciful and quite silly, for the Greek word is always the same.

Nonetheless, the point to ponder is that when we receive Christ as Saviour, we have *eternal* life. If life is really eternal, it is really eternal. If you can lose something which is eternal, then it was never really eternal in the first place.

2. Salvation is by grace, not by works. Ephesians 2:8-9, Titus 3:5, and other verses tell us that we can't earn salvation. Salvation is by God's grace, that is unmerited favor. Therefore, how can we lose unmerited favor? How can we lose that which is not deserved?

Of course, there are those who say that we get saved by grace, but in order to keep it we've got to "walk the straight and narrow." This is *exactly* what the Galatians were teaching (note Gal. 3:1-5 and 5:1). However, the exponents of this go right to Galatians 5:4 and say we can "fall from grace." *However, this verse is not saying anything about salvation. It is speaking of the Christian life.* By putting themselves under the law they had deprived themselves of the ministry of the Holy Spirit in their lives (note v. 5).

The Greek word for "fallen from" bears this out. The word *ekpipto* carries the idea of "losing one's hold." The Galatians had lost hold of the truth concerning the Holy Spirit's ministry in their lives. The entire context here *and* in Chapter 5 concerns the Holy Spirit's ministry. Therefore, "grace" is referring to the daily grace for living (given by the Holy Spirit) and this is the thing of which the Galatians were depriving themselves.

May we also add that just because the Galatians had "lost their hold" on God's truth, that doesn't mean God lost hold of them. *We* don't keep our salvation, just like the fact that we didn't attain it. *God keeps us.* He has hold of us. This leads to our next point.

3. God has the power to keep what He has saved. Without a doubt 1 Peter 1:3-5, John 10:27-29, and Romans 8:35-39 are among the strongest evidences for the security of the believer. Three different authors teach us the same truth.

First, we look at Peter's encouragement. He tells us in verses

3 and 4 of Chapter 1 of the inheritance that we have in Christ, which will not fade away nor wither, but rather is "reserved," that is "set aside, guarded," for us. Then we are told in verse 5 that we are "kept by the power of God." The word for "kept" is a military term meaning "to guard or protect." It is also a present participle showing continuous action which never ends. How marvelous all this is! While our inheritance is being guarded in *heaven,* we are being guarded on *earth* so we may be able to receive the inheritance. The guard is *never* absent, for the guard is God and He is always "on duty."

John then encourages us that we are God's sheep and He "knows" us. Again we see the verb in the present tense—action which is continuous, never ending. He continually knows us. He has given us *eternal* life and we, as the literal translation would be, shall "by no means" perish. Once we are in the watchful care of the Shepherd, *nothing* can destroy us nor snatch us from His care.

Then in that classic passage of Paul we see there is *nothing* that can "separate us from the love of God, which is in Christ Jesus our Lord" (Rom. 8:35-39). There are those who argue that nothing can separate us from God *except* ourselves. When we sin, we "sever ourselves" from God. However, this is just the point Paul is telling us that no created thing, including ourselves, can separate us from God's love. This is why "we are more than conquerors through Him that loved us." In addition, anyone who would say "I want to be severed from Christ" (as I have heard some argue) was never saved. How could a *true* child of God say or even think of such a thing?

Again, the main point to grasp is that it is *God's* power that keeps us, not our power. Those who deny the security of the believer are not grasping this truth. It is not what *we* do, but what *God* does.

4. The principle of justification. We often hear this defined as "just as if I never sinned." Well, that is not the case. We *have* sinned and nothing can happen which will alter this fact. In reality justification is "a judicial act whereby God declares us righteous." We, who are sinners, are declared righteous because the penalty of our sin has been paid by Jesus.

It is quite instructive to notice in the majority of texts where the word "justified" is used (Rom. 5:1, 9; Gal. 2:12, second usage; 3:24; Titus 3:7) the verb is in the aorist tense showing a once-for-all "declaring righteous." In a couple of texts, however, the verb is in a present tense (Rom. 3:24, 28) showing a continuous "declaring righteous." However, this causes no problem. In fact, it is quite marvelous. Not only does God do the work once-for-all, but He also continues doing the work. The thought is not that we are in a "process" of being justified, but rather we are constantly in the "state" of being justified. God has justified us and keeps us justified.

5. The principle of eternal redemption. Herein is a point of great blessing. The thing we must realize about the redemption of Christ is that *Christ died only once for each individual* (Heb. 10:10, 12, 14). We emphasize this so strongly because since Christ only died once for every person, therefore, each person can only be saved once. Hebrews 6:4-6 is a "problem passage" to some and a "proof passage" to others. The passage is quite simple in the light of Hebrews 10:10, 12 and 14. Since Christ died only once for our sin, then if someone *did* "fall away" (which is impossible), then it would then be impossible for him to be saved.

It is tragic that many today believe they can be saved one moment and lost the next and can get saved over-and-over again. However, this "crucifies Christ afresh and puts Him to an open shame." Beloved, this must not be!

6. The principle of sanctification. Akin to the above point is this one on sanctification. Look again at Hebrews 10:10. The word for "sanctified" is the word which means "to set apart for God." It is vital that we understand the tense of the verb, for it is in the perfect tense. This tense shows action in the past with an emphasis on the result. For example, when one gets married, there is a once-for-all action. However, the emphasis now is that he is still married. The action itself doesn't continue but the result does.

With this firmly established in our minds, let us realize that we are totally and completely set apart from sin and unto God once-for-all and are forever in that state. This is called "positional sanctification." There is then another attitude of sanctification called "practical sanctification." This is the day-to-day holy living which is the *result* of our position. We need to stay away from the idea of what is called "progressive sanctification," for this gives the idea that we keep getting holier and holier until someday we get completely holy. The thing we must realize is that we are completely holy *now*. I did not say we are perfect or sinless, for we still sin when we allow the flesh (Rom. 7) to rule, but we do not have to sin. God has set us apart from sin and unto Himself. We are no more holy today than yesterday. We merely live *out* what God has done *within*.

I urge the reader to read Dr. J. Sidlow Baxter's trilogy on this subject. Those three books are, *A New Call to Holiness, His Deeper Word in Us,* and *Our High Calling.* These are without doubt the most important works on this subject in the history of Christian literature.

7. The sealing of the Holy Spirit. In Ephesians 1:13 and 4:30 Paul tells us that we have been "sealed with the Holy Spirit of promise (1:13) "unto the day of redemption" (4:30). This one truth alone should bring perfect peace about the security we have in Christ. In both verses the aorist tense is used showing a once-for-all, never to be repeated action. It pictures the sealing of a letter by an official stamp so that no one will tamper with it until it gets to the one to whom it is addressed. We are sealed *permanently* until we are presented to Christ as His chaste bride (2 Cor. 11:2).

Moreover, the Holy Spirit is actually the seal itself! When we receive Christ as Saviour the Holy Spirit comes into us to indwell us (1 Cor. 6:19, Rom. 8:9-15) and to "baptize us," that is, "place us into" the Body of Christ as 1 Corinthians 12:13 and its context clearly show. Think of it! We are permanently sealed by the Spirit's presence in us!

8. Christ's intercessory work. The "finished" work of Christ was His death and resurrection, but His "unfinished" or "continuing" work is His intercession between us and the Father. This work is that of Christ coming to our defense when we commit acts of sin. The texts on this subject are Hebrews 9:24, 10:21-22; 1 John 1:9; and 2:1.

We should at this point carefully distinguish "habitual sin" from "an act of sin." This one contrast is why so many people do not grasp this truth of the believer's security. The phrase, "If any man sin" (1 John 2:1) is in the aorist subjunctive. The aorist tense is once-for-all action and the subjunctive mood is action which can possibly happen. The best way to express the subjunctive mood is with the word "if." Therefore, the best translation of this phrase is, "if any man commit an act of sin." It speaks of an act of sin, not continuous sin. John is showing us here that sin in the believer's life is infrequent, not habitual.

To go along with this, read 1 John 3:6. It literally says, "whosoever abides in Him does not habitually practice sin." Here we have the present tense showing continuous action. The man who is truly in Christ, truly born again, does not live in sin. The rest of the verse tells us, "whosoever sinneth hath not seen Him, neither known Him." The man who is continually sinning, who habitually sins over and over and who has no remorse for his sin shows that *he is not born again.*

Note one more verse in 1 John, Chapter 3, verse 9. Again, literally rendered, it tells us that "whosoever has been born of God does not habitually commit sin, for His seed continually remains in him and he cannot habitually sin, because he has been born of God." One who has been truly "born of God" (once-for-all act) cannot habitually commit sin. The words "his seed" refer to the divine life the believer possesses. This seed of divine life remains in us continually and makes it impossible for us to continually live in sin. God's seed causes us to hate sin and love righteousness.

Not only do these verses show the security we have in Christ since His seed is in us continually, but they also do great damage to the viewpoint that Christians have a "license to sin." It also does further damage to those dear Christians who reject the security of the believer because they think that anyone who believes in "eternal security" believes in a license to sin. They say, "Once you people are saved, you're always saved so you can do what you want to do." Not so! John tells us that a man who commits sin habitually and continuously day-in and day-out with no sorrow nor consciousness of sin, is lost—he was never saved. However, a man who has truly been born again no longer lives in sin.

Another question many ask on this subject is, "Well, how about the man who was saved but then 'backslid' for many years by going back to the old life?" According to the Scriptures, that man was never saved. Habitual sin shows a lost condition. This is the whole point of verses such as Romans 6:1-2, 2 Corinthians 5:17, and Titus 2:11-12. When a man comes to

Christ there *is* a change. There *must* be a change. If not, the man has not come to Christ.

All this brings us back to the intercessory work of Christ. Back in 1 John 2:1, we see that if we do commit an *act* of sin, not habitual but an act, we then have "an Advocate with the Father, Jesus Christ the righteous." How often do we have a wrong attitude, a wrong motive, a selfish desire, or say a cross word, or do something else which is displeasing to God. These are the realities in the life of every believer and are not habitual, continuous sin, but single acts of sin which happen when the Holy Spirit does not have control of our minds and bodies.

Dear Christian, when you sin, and it grieves your heart, or when you read God's Word or hear it preached, and realize there is something in your life which does not belong there, it is because you are "born of God." When there is sin in your life, it grieves your heart and pricks your spirit because the Spirit of God is in you. This does not happen to the "habitual sinner," because he is lost. However, it does happen to the true believer. It is then that we are to apply 1 John 1:9. The Greek word for "confess" is *homologeō, homo* meaning "same" and *log* meaning "word." Therefore, to confess means to say the same words about sin that God does. In other words, call sin *SIN.* Don't water it down. Call it what it is. It is only when we truly and sorrowfully confess our sin that God then forgives us.

It is at this time, when the believer commits an act of sin, that he has an "Advocate with the Father, Jesus Christ the righteous." The "advocate" is the Greek *paraklētos,* where we get the English word paraclete. It means, "one who is called alongside to aid." It is Jesus who is our paraclete, our "defense attorney," who comes to our aid when we commit an act of sin. It was Jesus, who, through His work on calvary, gave forgiveness of sin. It was Jesus, who by His death, burial and resurrection, gave us victory over the *penalty* and *power* of sin.

If we reject the security of the believer, we make all of this we have seen of no value. If we reject this doctrine we make Christ's intercession a waste of time and energy. In fact, if this doctrine of the believer's security is not true, then there is no intercessory work of Christ and to say that would be heresy.

9. God's children are *never* condemned. In John 3:18, we are told that those who believe in Christ are "not condemned," but

those who do not believe are "condemned already." The contrast in the verbs is most amazing. Those who believe in Christ are "continually not condemned," as the *present* tense indicates. This continuous action shows we will never be condemned. On the other hand, those who do not believe are once-for-all condemned and that condemned state will continue, as the *perfect* tense indicates. Those who are saved are never condemned, but those who are lost continue in condemnation. Since we are *never* condemned, then we must never be able to lose our salvation, for we then would be condemned again.

10. The Word of Christ to the lost. Those who reject the security of the believer are unaware that their position carries a very simple and subtle inconsistency. When the lost of the world stand before the Lord, He will say to them, "I never knew you; depart from me, ye that work iniquity" (Matt. 7:23). He will not say to them, "I used to know you, but you fell away," but rather "I *never* knew you. You have never belonged to me."

11. God has given us the way to *know* we are saved. In addition to what we have already examined in 1 John, there are a few additional points worth noting. Over thirty times John refers to *knowing* we are saved and he speaks of two kinds of knowledge. One is *ginōskō*, "to know by experience." The other is *oida*, "to know by learned facts." Using both of these, John says, we can know beyond any doubt that we are saved.

To understand John's First Epistle, one must understand his Gospel and the way they both relate. John's Gospel records seven miracles which are signs of Christ's incarnation and prove He is the Son of God, God in the flesh. By reading John 20:30 and 31 we find that the purpose of the Gospel was so we might believe in Christ and have eternal life.

Now, the reason John wrote his first epistle was so we might not just *have* eternal life by believing, but rather that we may *know* we have eternal life. The Epistle supplements the Gospel. It is the personal application of the Gospel. God not only wants us to have eternal life, He also wants us to know we have it! Let us look at a few instances here in 1 John.

In Chapter 2, verse 3, the word *ginōskō* is used, to know because we have personally experienced it. The first instance is in the *present* tense, to continually know. The second instance is in the *perfect* tense, past action with the emphasis on the result. Here is the blessing! "We continually, progressively know by experience that we came to know Him by experience in the past and are in that state right now." We must add also that "continuing in His commandments" don't "keep us saved." John points out that keeping God's commands are an *evidence* that we are indeed continuing in Christ.

Note then Chapter 3, verse 14. Here is a tremendous verse! Again, this is a *ginōskō* knowledge in the present tense. In addition, the word "abideth" is in the present tense and the word "given" is in the aorist tense. Putting all this together we see that "we continually know that He continually remains in us because of the Spirit that He gave us once-for-all."

Chapter 4, verse 13, is quite similar except the word "give" (referring to the Holy Spirit) is this time in the perfect tense. Therefore, "we continually know by experience that He continually remains in us because He gave us His Spirit once-for-all to remain in us permanently."

Then in Chapter 5, verse 13, we have action which is *possible.* It is possible that we may keep on knowing (present tense). The reason this action is only possible, not definite, is because it is based upon our decision. We *can* continually know, if we *want* to know. Note also that we may know *we have,* (present tense again), putting it together, "we can continually know that we continually have salvation."

The knowledge spoken of is the *oida* type of knowledge, knowledge gained, not by experience, but by someone teaching it to us or through other study. "The things (referring to the things concerning Christ) have been *written.*" We can read them and see God prove to us that we have eternal life.

12. The Principle of Adoption. Please note Romans 8:15-17. After reading these verses carefully, look also at Galatians 4:5 and Ephesians 1:5. The word "adoption" is the translation of the Greek word *huiothesia* which simply means "the placing of a son." It, therefore, speaks of our position as a child of God. Adoption can be defined as: "The placing of a son, who is not a son by birth, and giving him the place and inheritance of a son by birth." Dr. C. I. Scofield presents a marvelous comparison between regeneration and adoption: "In regeneration a Christian receives the *nature* of a child of God; in adoption he re-

ceives the *position* of a son of God" (The New Scofield Reference Bible, p. 1272—emphasis mine). So, we see that we are in the family of God through the merits of Jesus Christ, our Elder Brother (Rom. 8:29). We, who were once "of our father the devil" (as Jesus said of the Pharisees in John 8:44), are now part of God's family.

However, does this mean that when we sin we are "kicked out of the family," or otherwise disowned or disinherited? Indeed not! This is no more true in this spiritual sense than it is in the earthly sense. When we were children we did not cease being our parent's children when we disobeyed them. On the contrary, as erring children we were disciplined, but we were still their children. And, as we have already seen, this fact doesn't give us a "license to sin," for we know that as erring children we will be disciplined.

* * * * *

We could go farther, but we shall stop here. There are those who fear this doctrine of security; others just hate it. However, it should neither be feared nor hated. It should be loved, for it protects those who are *truly* born again; while, at the same time, it exposes and condemns those who are not truly saved. My prayer is that God's people will lay hold on the truth that God keeps us by *His* power, not ours, and that He wants us to live in response to that power.

Appendix II
The Christian's Library
(A reprint of a tract by the author)

It has been the burden of this writer for some time of the apparent increase in the lack of biblically oriented reading among Christians. This is due to many reasons too numerous to dwell on at present. The main point to grasp is that Christians must take time to read. Can we honestly say that the time we spend in secular reading is equalled by the time we spend reading the Bible and other Christian books? The only way we are going to grow in Christ is by reading. It is for this reason that the following lists have been compiled. The reader will notice that numbers follow many of the books listed. The number corresponds with a well-known Christian leader, author, speaker, and so forth, or other evangelical Christian leaders known personally by this writer. The list of contributors appears later. It is a sincere desire that these lists will greatly aid Christians in knowing more of the Saviour as we "give attendance to reading, to exhortation, to doctrine" (1 Tim. 4:13).

I. Devotional Aids

These are the foundational tools of your reading.

1. The Bible—Whether you read the Bible through in a year (about four chapters a day) or read a shorter portion, make sure you read it daily. There are many plans available to help, but never allow a *plan* to overshadow the *purpose.*

2. *The Imitation of Christ*—Thomas Kempis. For five hundred years the most widely read book of Christian devotions in the world. A classic.

3. *Awake My Heart*—J. Sidlow Baxter. A truly marvelous book of daily devotions. Destined to be a classic.

II. Twelve Essential Books

In addition to those above, here are twelve books which every Christian should read and make a part of his life:

1. *Balancing the Christian Life*—Charles Ryrie (1, 9)
2. *He That Is Spiritual*—Louis Sperry Chafer (1)
3. *Knowledge of the Holy*—A. W. Tozer (6)
4. *A Survey of Bible Doctrine*—Charles Ryrie (1)
5. *Going Deeper*—J. Sidlow Baxter (7)
6. *The Holy Spirit*—Charles Ryrie (*The Holy Spirit* by R. A. Torrey) (5)
7. *Sense and Nonsense About Prayer*—Lehman Strauss
8. *Great Bible Themes*—Louis Sperry Chafer (Authors 1 and 2 recommend Chafer's *Systematic Theology*—presented here is a simplified and concise work by Chafer).
9. *Dispensationalism Today*—Charles Ryrie (1, 2)
10. *Christian Holiness: Restudied and Restated*—J. Sidlow Baxter (Three volumes in one — also available in three separate volumes: *A New Call to Holiness, His Deeper Work in Us,* and *Our High Calling*)

III. Other Important Volumes

Among many others here are a few additional books which are of great value.

1. *The Romance of Redemption*—M. R. DeHaan (4)
2. Self-study Guides for Study—(Examples: Irving Jenson's Self-study Guides, or Ray Baughman's Bible Course (6)
3. Biographies of missionaries and other Christian leaders (6)
4. *Things To Come*—J. Dwight Penecost (2)
5. *The Rapture Question*—John Walvoord (1, 2)
6. *The Millennial Kingdom*—John Walvoord (1, 2)
7. *Mere Christianity*—C. S. Lewis (3)
8. *Christianity Through the Centuries*—Earle Cairns (5)
9. *The Divinity of Our Lord*—Canon Liddon (5)
10. *The Person and Place of Jesus Christ*—P. T. Forsyth (5)
11. *Know Why You Believe*—Paul Little
12. *Full Assurance*—Harry Ironside
13. *Does God Still Guide?*—J. Sidlow Baxter
14. *Fundamentalism and the Word of God*—J. I. Packer
15. *Rethinking Our Priorities*—J. Sidlow Baxter
16. *Preaching and Preachers*—D. Martyn Lloyd-Jones
17. *The Sermon on the Mount*—D. Martyn Lloyd-Jones
18. *Westminster Pulpit*—Sermons of G. Campbell Morgan
19. *Grace*—Louis Sperry Chafer
20. The *Be . . .* series of books by Warren W. Wiersbe
21. *Knowing God*—J. I. Packer

IV. Study Aids

These books are some basic aids to deeper study of the Word.

1. *Explore the Book*—J. Sidlow Baxter (5, 6; also highly recommended by Warren Wiersbe)
2. *Unger's Bible Handbook*—Merrill Unger (1, 2, 7)
3. *Unger's Bible Dictionary*—Merrill Unger (5) or *Wycliffe Bible Dictionary* (4)
4. Scofield Reference Bible (2)
5. Ryrie Study Bible (2)
6. Nave's Topical Bible (4, 7)
7. *Wuest's Word Studies*—Kenneth Wuest (7)
8. *Vine's Expository Dictionary of New Testament Words*—W. E. Vine (4, 7)

9. *Strong's Exhaustive Concordance*—(5) or *Young's Analytical Concordance* (2, 7)
10. *Everyman's Bible Commentary Series*—Various authors (1)
11. *Matthew Henry's Commentary Series* (3)
12. *Wycliffe Bible Commentary* (2)
13. *Barnes' Notes,* Tyndale Series, or Harry Ironside Commentaries.
14. *Manners and Customs of the Bible*—James M. Freeman or or a simpler work *The Way It Was in Bible Times*—Merrill T. Gilbertson

ors

and professor of Systematic al Seminary.

hor and president of Dallas

professor at Regent College.

:.

.

astor.